ACKNOWLEDGEMENTS

I would like to thank the following for allowing me to reproduce poems which they initially commissioned, broadcast, or published: *The Socialist Review, The Times Educational Supplement, The Times, The Independent, India Today, India Abroad, The New Statesman, The Observer, The Sunday Times of India, Staple, Raw Edge, Hope International, The Birmingham Post, The Radio Times,* City of Birmingham's Department of Recreation and Library Services, Buckingham Palace, Waterhall Gallery, Birmingham Rep, BBC Radio 4, BBC Radio 5, the Archaeological Museum in Lima, Taj Mahal National Trust of India, and the Indian High Commission.

I would also like to thank my previous publishers for their support: Charles Green Education and Publishing, Chronicles of Disorder Press, Castle View Publications, the Orange Studio, and UCE Press.

I would also like to thank my family and friends for their continued encouragement, namely my mother, my brother and sister, my son, Suneil, especially my friend Lynne Simmonds, who has spearheaded many of my projects and spent so long arranging this book, Laura Parfitt at Unique Broadcasting Company, colleague John Kirk, in UCE Enterprise at the University of Central England, for his support and sponsorship, and finally my fiancée, Samina Liaquat, for putting up with so many of my rants about poetry.

I am also indebted to the Arts Council of England (West Midlands Region) for their partial funding of my post.

First published in 2004
by
UCE Press
University of Central England
Perry Barr, Birmingham B42 2SU
United Kingdom
Distributed by Marketing Unit

Typeset by L. Simmonds

Printed by Cromwell Press Ltd
Aintree Avenue, White Horse Business Park, Trowbridge
Wiltshire, BA14 0XB

A CIP record for this book is available from the British Library

ISBN 0904354806

Illusions and Delusions and Dirty Words

Selected Poems and Prose
1994 - 2004

ROSHAN DOUG

UCE Press
England

By the same author:

DELUSIONS
Charles Green Education (1995)

…THICKER THAN WATER
(Pamphlet with Wayne Dean-Richards)
Chronicles of Disorder Press (1998)

THE ENGLISH-KNOWING MEN
Castle View Publications (1999)

NO, I AM NOT PRINCE HAMLET
The Orange Studio (2002)

THE DELICATE FALLING OF A GOD
UCE Press (2003)

In memory of my father Shri Gurbachan Doug
(1930-2004)

CONTENTS

No I Am Not Prince Hamlet

Illusions and Delusions and Dirty Words

Whispers

They're
confiding thoughts in secret whispers
hush-back words that falsify their
feelings, intricately colliding
with an imaginary world.

I
sit, subdued, inert, perpetuating a claim
that poets don't see, don't hear
wrapped in a literary world
of illusions and delusions and dirty words.

Delusions

Rain on my Universe

Rain on Rahoon falls softly, softly falling,
Where my dark lover lies.
Sad is his voice that calls me, sadly calling,
At grey moonrise.
James Joyce, She Weeps Over Rahoon, 1912

For a while I stood and stared at the rubble that lay at the entrance of our old school, *caput mundi*. They were knocking it down to make space for a car park and public conveniences.

It was afternoon.

The sky was a Presbyterian blue with a rainbow stretching high. Raindrops had fallen only minutes before but now I thought how unusually warm it was for autumn after a chilly summer, typically wet. I eventually walked into the playground, placing the helmet comfortably on my head. 'Just in case something falls', the workman said, gently cautioning me.

Everything was still; a moment captured in time. The painted target we used for shooting practice was still there, though some of the colours had been scrapped and others were fading with the sun and the rain. The Physics lab was also standing above the workshop where I made a spatula for my mother the day she had lost her baby but I didn't know.

'Kevin has made a table and you're still cutting that piece of wood. Wha'ch yer been doin' – day-dreaming?'

And the graffiti my friend had epitaphed echoed to me as he stood leaning with brassy masculinity against the toilet wall. 'School is a load of piss and shit', he wrote. 'And when I die I want to be remembered for this'. And we thought how funny it was but I noticed his eyes were inert, vaguely sad. 'Beats your poetry any day,' he joked and I smiled and said, 'Yes'.

I walked along the elongated wall to the bottom of the playground, through the rubble and the sand. The times we played here, fought, lost and bled and the dreams had all fled.

'I can't wait to leave this place'.
'Nor me.'
'There must be more to life than this.'
'There's got to be,' I said.

And I stood alone with emptiness lingering all around me. And I thought of the day when I went to visit him. Curtains were still drawn and I thought it was strange for two o'clock on a hot summer's afternoon. And no-one said anything at school, my universe. Infinite galaxies collided, died and were born again but we said nothing. Not a word. And I remembered how nothing can come of nothing.

How a farewell is always necessary.

For a moment space was tranquil perfectly still. The oak and the willow behind the perimeter wall had been cut to make way for a new estate. Not a breeze was in the air; the sky was motionless. And then on the lawn of one of the houses I caught sight of an old woman hanging the washing on the line, dressed in black, not white – a Punjabi dress cut far too loose as it waved in the returning breeze. Her eyes were sunken, sullen and deep and I thought of Mr King and the Reverend Burnell. In the background I heard an Indian song, faint, serene and mournful but no music came therein. And I thought it was odd; a black dress, a sunny sky and a song bereft of music.

And a voice calling me, in the echo of the yard, in the pain of the ruins.

I gazed across the main school building, squinting my eyes (my sight isn't what it used to be). And I thought of you, and the autumnal sky when you held my hand and whispered you loved me. And I smiled and said that I loved you too. Then we held each other and kissed, and you asked if we'd always be together and I promised we would. I promised too much. I didn't think that time and space would move.

'Sorry, mate', the workman said, moving the bulldozer close.

Shifting I walked to the entrance. The acrylic blue doors had been torn apart, forcibly; one of them as plastered with a Union Jack and had been stowed onto a skip. The classroom was there. And I remembered what he did to you inside. You came onto him he said, tempting him. And you told me about your mother through your tears. I told you not to worry, and then you got married and left. And as I stood I saw images of your wedding, your husband, your baby – and your son born quietly in the dark, secretly into this world. Not a card was sent, not a whimper. Just two silent lonely tears staring at the altar in the temple.

Not a word; not a touch.

Slowly my heart started to swoon as the rain began to fall from a clear sky. I felt betrayed as I looked up, fooled once again. The universe was so vast, so empty. Our galaxy was just one in a million, a billion. Insignificant. I thought of babies and temples, groups of people hurled together. There were gas chambers, castes and classes. And I thought of country churchyards, effigies on tombstones and the epitaph on his grave with fungus growing inside next to a gentle stream. Images concurred in my mind of dust and ashes, of funeral pyres flickering against a solitary sky but always in the background there's you, plain and silent. Always there's you, whispering through the leaves, the wind in its listlessness.

Speak kindly.

My clothes were damp and warm as I looked at our school for the last time, to capture the image forever. The arched windows were boarded up, so cold and damp and true. The roof had been ripped bare, now a frame, timber of what used to be; a building of our past, a remnant of a piece that was yours, that was mine, that was you. Old and dilapidated it stood, a reminder that finality is.

'You alright?' the workman asked as I handed him the helmet. 'Yes, fine', I replied and I walked over the rubble that lay underneath my feet thinking of the grave, the woman, the song and you. And with the sun and the rain I walked through the sand and dust and ashes. Sand to rubble and dust to dust and my ashes.

You, the Night and I

Soundly I lie
with the clock ticking by
it's 12.15 on a winter's night
when all the wives are asleep
not unlike me and true,
not you.

Your books are open
paper sprawn all over the floor
and your typewriter, I hear,
is clicking, moving the big world.

In the dark, I make plans
and dream on
while you make up words.

Moth in the Night

Beside the clock, the moth
was circling our lamp shade
when I woke last night. You lay
unstirring and I

thought it was odd that
my shuffle didn't wake you,
as it once did.
Your breasts soft and saggy

coiled underneath you, deep
inside, and I gazed
at the images on your face
lines I did not see

when we met. I could not
sleep. So after I'd pissed I
sat and read the letters
you had written.

Words were lost somewhat,
crinkled, and a tear sat
between us like poetry.
And a time, a past with commas

and short pauses, separated
us, not a sound, not a grunt
not a fear in the room:
just a bleak emptiness of a grave yard –

the motion of a stream. And when I
climbed back to you, the clock

13

ticked in the hollowness, the lamp
stood but the moth had gone.

Breaking Glass
(for my brother)

My brother was sevenish
when he put a fist into our front window
and drenched our door with blood.

The kids were making fun of him
calling him names and I joined in.
We said he was a sissy
'cause someone had beaten him up.

But when the window shattered
and the pieces fell to the concrete ground
all I could feel was the sound,
the hurt, the tears in his face
and anger burning inside him.

My father didn't punish him
instead he praised him and said
he was spirited.
I thought it was odd but I couldn't
help looking up at my brother
even though he was smaller than me.

So now when I speak to my father
I wish it had been me
who had broken that window.

Class One

She was like my mother
unlike Mrs Sainsbury who took
my hymn book because I couldn't sing to music.

But Dawn Scott let me share hers
then sat next to me for a whole year.
Once she gave me a packet
of *Walkers* cheese and onion and in return
I allowed her a swig of my cola
(it had been intensely hot on the field).

She flicked her hair and took the brim
of the bottle to her lips and when
she gave it back to me
a faint line of cola had formed around her mouth
which she brushed
with the back of her hand.
She said I was like her brother.

I smiled but I couldn't
help staring at her light nylon blouse
through which I could see the outline
of her unfettered tits.

A Drink in the Canteen
(for a student)

In silence we smiled:
a cup of coffee and tea
united us, like the legend

of King Arthur at college.
It was break. She glanced
at me like a child,

innocently, and spoke of her
poetry and petals in the wind.
I was scared to probe deep,

I said nothing. Her words
and sentences led to him,
of storms in the rainbow

and the walk in the park. There
she was a work vandalised,
burgled at fifteen. Ejected now

with ink splattered on her form
thinking, forcing herself to translate
her thoughts, anger, her guilt

into words, like gentle rain
slowly washing away her stains.
And I thought of you once again,

your touch, the clock and the bed
and us, lying quietly. We were
mute then, as now. The conversation

had ended with a full cup
of tea, a lonely tear but still,
I could think of nothing to say.

A Crayon
(for Suneil)

A crayon dreams of wanting to be more
to become a pencil perhaps or even a pen

A crayon dreams of wanting to be more
than the tedious random movements of a child
than the uncertainties or the riddles of a teenager

A crayon dreams of wanting to be more
than the mere colours of red, white and blue
to be a leader of his people
to be a pacifist

A crayon dreams of exploring
the difficult shades of grey
to be held by the artist by a sunny stream
to be more than a poet's rhyme
more than chalk that turns to dust
or ink that fades in time

A crayon dreams of wanting to be more
more than a wish of life
more than the depth of its sleep
a crayon dreams endlessly
and even a crayon wants more than this.

Barish

It's the sound of the rain
crashing against my window
that wakes me
in the middle of the night
at 12.15
not your voice that echoes
in my mind
effortlessly
a tune you've woven
through the heavy raindrops
falling;
and our child sleeping
snug as a pillow
warms me,
his face is a picture
you had
unselfishly created
and now
unhaunting me
in the background of my life
through the whish of the wind
of an endless grey
and in the sound of the rain
falling.

'Barish' Hindi meaning rain

The Rajai

the rajai I throw off
is called something
else as I switch on the box
like the rice I eat
with coconuts

books are killing me

the world in which
I move is
letters and images
interpreted eaten
half-heartedly

television was the key word

but my parents did not
realise it
now words are bullets
I use at them
standing still
I don't give them lip
I just watch TV

my world is spinning
my parents are not
my mum doesn't
understand me

her tears say it all
words meant everything
to me

but my father sees
nothing
he just sits
and watches the telly

whilst I hit the duvet
once more

'Rajai' Punjabi meaning a thick duvet

Welcome to Britain

Without reading they're burning his book
at Gandhi's funeral pyre

standing around in salwar and kameez
next to the 'Welcome to Britain'

sign at Terminal Three. They pronounce
in broken English that he

only has a few weeks to live. And
as they speak I wonder

if the followers from Sky will wear
Armani suits on Judgement

Day and I think of *Star Trek* and *Lassie*
and *Champion the Wonder Horse*

whilst faintly I can hear the 'Rivers of Blood'
speech. Ultimately I think of him.

But with his probing Britishness I'm sure
he won't make a big deal out of it.

She Wears a White Cloth

She wears a white cloth – one of mourning at a pyre
not the Christmas white that's
cheap and tacky and immoral –

as they parade around the fire
summoned by the mother
who has substituted compassion
and in rage crowns the Indian lies
she does not believe

and still she smothers as they go by
caressing the red silken sari

but in her daughter's face not a whimper nor glory
   lost
just a passive blankness empty of hope
her mind on other things –
echoes of the past kissing in her ears
the fingering of warmth inside –
in body and in form she moves

her heart on a being on a far off shore
not on the brothers she leaves behind
nor on the one who walks before.

The Last Moment
Do not go gentle into that good night,
Old age should burn and rave close of day;
Rage, rage against the dying of the light.
Dylan Thomas, 1952

I was informed through a relative of mine
that he died peacefully that night.
The doctor said it was the ward
that made noise, not his bed.
To think, twelve hours before I was there.

A day before I sat in awkward silence
outside a threatening sky of cloud and wind.
I couldn't think of a word to say:
no smile pursued from my lips, no comfort lay bare.
Like the trees I could see
over the brown railings, I was dead.

Twenty years had passed and returned to stand
between us.
Through the window I could hear the raindrops
but from his pillow not a sigh;
not a word of recognition – just a pitiful stare.
There he was flesh of my flesh, blood of my blood
a body of Indian air lying in front of me
and I could say nothing. I offered no alms.

The rain gushed down eventually
and I thought of frozen winters
of furnaces and ice, and memories poured,
memories of my actions, of my failure,
memories of my pen he had bought for me
when I took the examinations at sixteen.
And I thought of what he wanted – a dream

25

but now there I was: nothing of recognition;
nothing to smile about; nothing achieved.

So when his eyes fell, I rose
and looked at his face.
It was no longer the plain face I knew,
it was mapped, a map I had drawn
with every line and knot now wrinkling,
a strained neck upon strained arms.
I swept my fingers along his palm
a touch that once awoke him
in the morning with only half my love
and I walked away

quietly, into the cold air,
the dark sky, and the rain falling.

The Epitaph

What will be on my epitaph
I often ask myself
and who will
read it
or care
or bear the thought
of me
in there
who will sit
by it and kiss
who will smother it
with his piss
who will bark
in the dark
or craft
his art
or kick his ball
against my wall
who will care
if I loved
or sang
or wrote
some poems
that no-one
has read
or who will gaze
and spare a thought
with worms
on my face
who will toddle
to bed
work themselves

hot red
and think of their jobs
the mobs
who rob
and remember
a Fred
who said
something to Ed
God! Life is so dead!
and while I sleep
the earth will
rotate
the stars
operate
the universe will
inflate
isn't it great
to leave a trace
on such a place

with me in my bed
no sound in my head
only my son
will say
'Poor sod, he's dead'.

In the Darkness of my Room

In the darkness of my room I dream
My conscience does not let me sleep
It does not rest: it will not set me free
The voices I hear, and pictures I see
Are sights and sounds of yesteryear
From a summer's day, that was not to be
And yet the warmth I felt is still with me.

So alone I sit in the darkness of my room
Our son lying still, peacefully, like a winter's moon –
Blissfully ignorant and innocent of all that's true
But in his face, I still see you
You're the emblem of love, the symbol of truth
Forever constant, forever on the move
Caressing the solitude, in the darkness of my room.

Sleep Walk

I stood in the garden last night. The weeds are growing again. The roses you planted are out. And as I cut off the stems I pricked my forefinger just as I had done when you were here. And I sucked and remembered you holding me on the bench on Broad Street, lovingly, soothingly. Do you remember when I cut my finger? Part of you is still here in this garden, in our bedroom where our son lies peacefully. But you're so far away, so close. Only silence separates us as I imagine you, him and the bed. I can neither see nor feel anything, nothing of comfort. Just the warmth of a summer's night and the distance of the stars. The blood, the moon and the stars and Diwali looming in the skies. Sunshine will follow rain. Sunshine follows rain.

Brighton

I see Brighton, when I look out
not my room of darkness
of reflections
of thoughts
of time and space that once was
still and clear
a time that meant all to me
of space that you
have made your own

I see Brighton, when I look out
when I walk the streets
of Handsworth, not our school
not the library
or the University Park
not the rivers or the lakes
not our talks
of our dreams in the car

I see Brighton, when I look out
not your caresses nor your tears
not the visits to the temple
your house
the hospital
with our hearts full of fears

I see Brighton,
not the warmth of your touches
not your confessions, not your smiles
not your blushes

I see Brighton, when I look out

not the colours of the night
but a light that lived for a flicker of life
the sadness lingers on, you see
and the sadness entwines in my dreams
my unconscious sleep
of silence
and betrayal
of you and me

I see Brighton all around
cynics, pregnancies,
would-be mothers crying quietly alone
for a child they did not see
in clinics far away –
dying as he enters the light

Brighton

My conscience tears at me
I will never be free,
so now I see Brighton
I see Brighton all around me.

Dialogue with a Poet

Why do you write?

Because of love
Because of words
>of wine
>of flowers
>of silk

Because of sunsets
>over the mountains
>the music
>in the rain

Because of poetry

Bullshit!

I write because I can
>I do
>I have
>nothing in this world
>that is mine.
>Sometimes
>I hate
>words
>and commas
>and pauses
>that make
>no sense at all,
>they make me feel
>trapped
>a failure
>a disaster
>a shit

in my father's world

I write because of conflicts
of muscles
of pens
of books
of images
in my head
contorted
when I write
contorted
when I speak
a world
that is lost
an ocean
that moves
mountains
that rise

I write because I'm screwed
I have nothing
to say
that means
anything
to you
or to me
words are something
I dream
I rape
I lie
I steal
I cheat
in the class
in the playground
where a dead man

lies
a tramp
shot in the head
it's me

I write because of women
of breasts
of softly fondled
tits
because of God
the devil
the bastard doesn't exist!

I write because of darkness
of dreams
of nightmares
in my sleep
writing communicates
a voice
I speak
I think, of her
touch
her face
Helen of Troy
moves me
slowly
silently
to a rush
to anger
to guilt
of losing
of joy
of tears
of a pompous man
brooding

I write because I'm vain

            vanity
            rules me
            to a hush
            the pen
            washes away
            my sins
            and art
            is killing me
            and that
            is why you see
            that is why I write
            that is why I write
            you see.

Friday Night

the holy committee sat with their back
towards the altar and the cross

discussing the day's takings and politics
when I walked in to use

the toilet. No-one noticed me, my smoke-
filled jacket, beer breath or shoes.

The urinal was stained with silence and a cigarette
butt floated on my piss while I

read the graffiti *'Maj is the biggest slag'*
and I wondered if the magi

had also fist-fucked to sleep. After the
climax the butt was covered. I didn't

feel pleasure or relief just the darkness of the night
the cold emptiness as I walked out

to my car, to the waiting white woman, smiling
alone with her freshly glossed lips.

Point of Redemption

To know how to free oneself is nothing;
the arduous thing is to know what to do with one's freedom.
André Gide, The Immoralist, 1902

It is the beginning. Darkness turns to light. Not a sound. Not a word. Not a guru.

One day a Hindu man is out walking in the desert. It is very real. He is thin. He has been walking for quite some time. He is weary and thirsty. So, he stops and sits and leans against a wall.

A few minutes later he realises he hadn't noticed the wall before. He looks up. It is not a very tall wall. He looks across. It is endless both ways. He looks back at the path he had followed. It is not there anymore. There is no-one around, apart from the dead bodies lying beside the wall. 'How will I get back to my mother?' he thinks. He takes out his note pad and begins to write: *'One becomes a Brahmin not by birth but by deed'.*

He pauses and thinks for a while. It is strange that there should be this wall in the middle of the desert. How absurd! As he contemplates he begins to hear a sound behind the wall, a sound of a waterfall. He presses his ear against the wall and the sound is even more clear. It pleases him. He turns to his note pad and continues to write. *'Mother have you built this wall?'* He sits and night falls.

The next morning he is awoken by the sound of birds singing on the other side of the wall. It pleases him. It is very real. He looks around and thinks, 'Maybe there's a door further along.' So he begins to walk along the wall, avoiding dead bodies on the floor. He walks for hours into the horizon. There is no door. Finally, he sits down. Weary and tired he sleeps. Night falls.

On the third day he awakes feeling very hungry. He looks around – only dead bodies he had seen before. They are real. He is real. There must be a reason. He contemplates, 'Maybe I could eat one of these bodies'. And forgetting his religion, he attempts to eat but his teeth are too weak. They cannot bite. 'It is futile,' he thinks. 'What can I do?' And he sits once more listening to the sounds of the waterfall and the birds singing on the other side of the wall. His eyes close. Darkness falls.

On the fourth day he is awoken by the sunlight as the sounds continue on the other side of the wall. It is hot. It is intense. It is very real. He looks up, a clear blue sky. Not a drop. And then in the distance, he sees a hill, a green hill far away with a cross. His mother crucified. He rises and begins to walk towards them. He runs, wobbles and falls. He looks up. The scene is not there anymore. It is unreal. He is not. He lies down and closes his eyes. Darkness. Night falls.

On the fifth day he awakes long before the sun appears in the sky. He does not move but stares at the ground upon which he lies. The sounds of the waterfall and the birds continue behind the wall. Yes, it is real. And then the green hill appears before his eyes once more. He sees his father crucified. His mother stands laughing. Surely it is real. He moves but falls hitting his head upon the ground. Some blood trickles from his head onto the hot sand. The sound of the waterfall stops. He cannot hear the birds any more. He lies watching, watching nothing. It is not unreal. Night falls.

On the sixth day he awakes but does not move. There is no sound. The wall is not there anymore and the dead bodies vanish into thin air. He sits up. The waterfall is there amongst a country green, in a country scene. Is it real? And the birds are there but no sound can be heard. He watches for a long time without moving. Convinced that his world is real, he slowly stands and steps towards the scene. But as he moves the wall appears once more and the dead bodies emerge on the floor. It is unreal. With tears in his eyes he sits and night falls.

On the seventh day he awakes to laughter on the other side of the wall. But he does not move because it could be real. He lies motionless. The wall disappears and the dead bodies vanish. He does not care. The waterfall appears the birds sing. Still he does not move. He remains motionless. It starts to rain. A cold trickle of water forms upon his face. The rain disappears. Still he does not move. He is content to die. He wants to die. He dies. Night falls.

Good night, mother
Good night, sweet mother
Good night, good night.

Thicker Than Water

Those Yearning Years

Upon his face I saw for years as he printed Urdu
strokes about going back when the kids have
    grown.

And then I'd scribble a foreign name and write
a familiar phrase 'wife of' or 'son of' followed by
    an inky

tribal surname, corrupted by the snow and the rain.
At times I posted those letters light as the Indian

Ocean to which I directed them. And my father
would explain the family tree, how we all fitted in,

and tell me who was who and in which village he
    lived,
pride and passion in his voice and a yearning to go
    back

home. And I'd imagine a far away world like
    Timbuktu
where a man's status was defined by the number of

buffaloes he had or acres under his name, not by
a simple degree from an odd university, locked
    away

in a drawer made of English Oak, an
    acknowledgement
rarely made, but an embarrassment all the same.

Sucrose-herbs

I was only four when my mother
began telling me stories of
Indian gods who were strong,
brave and spiritually powerful.
They protected the meek, our
kingdom and brought hope and
light to thick darkness. But
most of all they shielded
children like my would-be
brother. Later I often addressed
light blue air mail letters to
Village Post Office Rahimpur
where my unknown cousins all
lived. She would show me black
and white photos of them tattered
over the years and I would study
their blackened faces staring
at the lens with an uncomfortable
squint showing off their newly
made *shalwar* or *kameez*. They were
remote to me as the man on the
moon and just as silent: a land of
ghosts, dreams and goblins, I
thought. My writing was small,
careful and exact as I wrote
pronouncing their Indian names in
anglicized tones which never looked
the same on paper – just a corrupted
tongue and the bestest fonts colliding
with the strangest vowels and
consonants. And I remember coming
home one afternoon, the house was

scarred and silent. My mother
and her friend were sitting
on the linoleum floor with mat-
murasized tears and my aunt was
boiling tea with sucrose-herbs.
I didn't know what had happened,
but I noticed my mother didn't pray
for a couple of days and she never
told me stories of gods, who protected
new born babies, ever again.

Hain-Jee

The word I learnt to speak after bullshit was *Hain-
      Jee.*
My mother taught me and insisted I use it in my
speech, waddling my tongue every now and then,
setting a lingual mechanism. My father ignored all
      this,
too busy to stir, to concern himself with Indian
social niceties. His own diction short, brief and
      abrupt.

And now thirty years on he insists I speak it.
His words come flowing like oceanic tides, dark
      and
deep. 'I went to your *massey's* house, and all her
kids were using it. And you? You think you're
above that don't you with your university degree.'
Pages turn, books, words, a dry flower in my
      notebook.

And as he spouts drowning his bitterness with
      drink,
I remember a girl who said *Hain-Jee* to me,
quite accidentally, when I called out her name
during registration. But she didn't mean correct
and present but an acknowledgement of a shared
opaque ancestry defined by the colour of my skin
and name. Or was it just her parents' lingual
      conditioning?

Chalo

Chalo is a myopic word I have often heard in our
    household
growing up where chips were bought on Friday
    nights only.

It's not that my father was stingy, he always gave
    me two
ten pence pieces if I woke up dazed at five when he
    left

for the foundry, and he often bought us cheese and
    onion
crisps and *Vimto* from the pub in the evening. And
    many a

time we'd sit and watch wrestling on Saturday
    afternoon,
before Alan Towers read out the final score. *Dr
    Who* was

our favourite and the Daleks used to scare the pants
    off me.
And my father would ask what *sabjee* my mum
    was cooking

and then drink a glass or two of *Haig* or *Bells*
    whisky
(he could certainly take his drink) and with a wink
    of

an eye, he'd pour a proud innocent glass for me.
    Sometimes

he'd sit and tell us stories of how he used to walk
    four miles

to school, somewhere near the Himalayas crossing
    a live
perilous stream on the way. And he'd tell us how
    lucky

we were for our school was only a short innocuous
    distance
away (the irony now overwhelms me). And after
    some laughter

and jokes he'd slump on the settee for his weekly
    nap while
I would scrutinize his hands twice the size of mine
    and hard

as brittle, and brush his scar on his forehead
    plastered
prominently in Singapore before I was born in a
    life long

brotherly brawl. And tonight as I sit I can hear his
    chalo
calling me. But I have not the will or the strength
    to follow

his blood for the Severn and the Thames and the
    Ganges,
run like a blank verse, cascading between us.

Reading Comics and Metamorphosizing

It's almost Christmas, 1969
David Banner has just metamorphosized into Hulk.
I awake, dazed-scepter'd eyes, in the middle of the
    night,
dark as the snow outside and just as green.

It's a fantasy world I take to school
where I sit thinking of comic strips – Peter Parker
and Clark Kent. At times I interfuse the narrative
in my head with Steve Austin and actuality and
dissect my Maths equations with pictorial
    imaginings;
a powerful plot and complex figures, never quite
    moving.

Melodious sounds of hush-muffled hymns
noodle my descent upon the cold stairs
where incense floats through the wooden-spiral,
a serpent of cultural smoke and haze.

My mother is crouched making a coal fire
wearing a clumsy veil, a *chunni*, thin like tissue;
her hands are covered in ash –
the bloody thing doesn't start.
I switch on the telly to test-card music
folding my legs upon the torn settee.

We're incessantly mute and alien-like
as my father finishes with the *Wilkinson Blade,*
cold and blunt, and gulps a cup of tea. He smiles
and hands me a ten pence piece and packs

for the foundry, and the deadly snow,
upon which he casts neon shadows in the street,
falls, while I sit munching cornflakes, crunching;
my identity fusing with his *Des Pardes* weekly
and my *Spiderman* comics.

Fishing the Stars

Under the Northern Constellation we could have
    held our hands forever,
sitting at our lake, not daring to move in case we
    scared the piranhas
or the kingfishers. They were darting in and out of
    our cautious silence,
plopping every ripple, defined by an expansion of
    unspoken words and phrases.

Above the darkness, the moon was out, full and
    keen guiding the stars
unnaturally, not real or still yet turning the solar
    system inexplicably
like our thoughts or the mechanical beating of our
    hearts.
And like the stars, I pictured a Stanley knife and a
    Colt. 45 in San Francisco
and Uncle Ravi writhing in pain, a shot off face,
    torn bloody,
as if he'd been eaten by the piranhas in our lake.

The English-knowing Men

When England was English

It was late October, before Hallowe'en during my first year at our comprehensive when Old Bull, our English teacher, met a cantankerous new disease whose name in four words I couldn't pronounce or see; the week the pilot episode of *Starsky and Hutch* was shown on a starlit-night Friday, shortly after the *Nine O'clock News* when Ian McCaskill would blunder the weather forecast and the whirling globe was still a symbol of the people's BBC...

Back at school on Monday, our second period of the day, Old Bull was subdued with a faraway gaze not here nor there, like the multi-racial class that listened or not, talking in desultory tones of Saturday night and the Gran Torino – red with a lightning white stripe – action all the way. Geoffrey and Jawaid were punching each other in the back row like American cops, George was designing an aerodynamic plane and naming it 'Zebra Three', Winston was moaning to Alan for not being able to play football on Saturdays (against his religious beliefs) with only Parminder browsing at his *Six Million Dollar Man* cards, and, on the far side, a couple of plaited girls were glancing and giggling at Steve.

Oblivious in the midst of those separate worlds, those insulars of insularity, Old Bull, his eyes raw and sparkling, read us a piece by Dylan Thomas, a voice I couldn't work out, a look, a pause at every line: 'And death shall have no dominion.' Poetry came flooding, blank as a midnight sky, a vacuum in his own world. And suddenly, there he was, standing, tears and all, defiance without quite defying, his voice quivered faltering, a kind of dignity at his own indignity: 'And death shall have no dominion.' And one by one we fell to a hush, confusedly, complexity compounding, staring at the world turning upside down, a foundation crumbling all around me: 'And death shall have no dominion.' And then, abruptly, he stopped like time itself, like sickly breath, turning to the arched window remnant of Charles Dickens' Gradgrind's school of mid-nineteenth century Britain, when England was English and the Empire ruled the world. 'We're fools guided by the stars,' he spoke glancing at the morning clouds outside, 'moving us, pulling west always it seems.' And immediately I felt a sudden sharp thrust of sadness, injectory pain, like under a surgeon's knife, not knowing how or why, but feeling or seeing the fading away of something implicitly at an end, the ebbing away of life; pain that returned a few years ago when I read that Starsky's wife, Elizabeth, and children were also dying of AIDS, and that Paul and David never made it as cosmic stars like Stan Laurel, Paul Newman or Humphrey Bogart.

Playing with 007

Mr Pierris had kept Linton Small and Mark Joinson
   in
as detention for not grasping the fundamentals of
   Physics.

'Density equals mass over volume', he kept saying
   in an ethnic
colonial tone at odds with a modern comprehensive
   when

Steve Coppell was at Manchester United and
   Martin Buchan
was my hero. A time when I fantasized about
   being 007 or

the first Asian to play in Division One and score a
   Brazilian
goal at Wembley, when talks of India its shades
   and colours

still embarrassed me like the enunciated breasts of
   Miss Iliffe,
a time when we took the piss out of the Bengali
   lads

in group four who couldn't speak English quite like
   us
and didn't know the name of an English coach and
   never

read *Shoot*. And when Mark and Linton eventually
   came
out at four scratching their heads like a couple of

cartoon characters

we were having a half-time break and sharing a
    bottle
of *R. Whites' Lemonade.* I was in goal now and I
    noticed

how they played as if to compensate for their
    academic
failures. And Linton punched one of the Bengali
    kids

because he made a brilliant save next to the NF
    letters
on the toilet wall plastered deep in our conscience.
    And

no-one said anything, just sniggered as we watched
the goalie get up and leave, shaken but not stirred.

Eczema Revisited

He sits with a teddy on his lap
staring at the wall, a paradoxical sleepiness
that echoes my own.
The atlas lies beside him
(outline of a coast I've never seen).

He doesn't talk...
he listens, tentatively,
to a sound I haven't made...

twitching to scratch, to touch,
a paraesthetic experience.
The television buzzes...
pictures camouflaged in his mind,

darkness giving way to light...
and smiles instantly
when Donald Duck speaks...

squelching animatedly.

Facing the Truth with a Sioux Indian

When you are sorrowful, look again in your heart, and you shall see that in truth you are weeping for that which has been your delight.
Kahlil Gibran, The Prophet, 1923

A dark bush in front of us, full

It was a dry summer's evening, kind but unnatural –
the sky was a blaze of riots, bewildering as Machu
    Picchu
as I sat watching the sun descend over Cannon Hill
    Park.
Our son sat sucking on your favourite lollipop
oblivious to our world, aimless,
lost in his own

of horses, ducks and rabbits.

And I thought of you sitting underneath the willow
that had grown old and weeps like our memories,
like the thoughts of the Incas.
Your hands were soft, entwined in mine
and your head rested upon my shoulder
like the world you seemed to carry on your own.

A crackle of leaves, a scurry

We were perfect and silent like the *Mona Lisa*, we
    said
nothing, only the breeze, the slight teasing of the
    wind
spoke to us of our past and present, surreal almost,
absurd as the plight of the street children in Brazil.
A thousand words could not have expressed our

feelings
our thoughts so loving and mournful

a cautious twig, a stone, a squirrel.

And when you smiled a million stars seemed to
     shine
in your eyes; a million songs were sung; a million
poems were read; and for a moment, the universe
was your face: strange, complex and beautiful, loud
and silent it stood like a magnet, a speck in the
     desert
a Pole Star in the West.

It sniffs and picks and beams unaware of our
     eyes (our son smiles silently).

And when you planted a kiss on my forehead, it
     was not
the kiss of a girlfriend but a sharman, a calypso,
     whose
volcanic lips melted my soul. You were the closest
     and
the furthest spirit, the plainest and the ambiguous
     a sentence and a thesis,
an egotistical savage.

It's hiding now, darting, pausing now, darting

And I noticed there was lava in your eyes
but when I brushed it away your reply was the
     strangest
thing, 'This means nothing to me,' you said
shielding your eyes. 'I need the rain to wash me
     away,

I need the rain to wash me.'
The Amazon forest remains

invisible, there now, invisible,

I looked at our son staring at me, incredulously.
'It's gone, Dad. Where's it gone?'
'I don't know,' I replied facing the willow and the
    sycamore
tree sitting in a lost world like a visitor at a hospital
    bed
like a tourist
and the fading sun descending

touching light, darkness, death and dreams

The rain never did fall that summer, the driest on
    record
and when it did, it was after a Sioux Indian
danced in London late in October by which time
    you'd
gone unwashed of your sins, closing in dying,
    moving
like a black hole where the squirrel now hides,
    perpetually

and the dandelions dancing for us.

Kay

Kay, almost as if the *ay*
didn't exist
a denigrated deviation of *clay*
where life springs
biblical yet puzzling,
like a foreign word
meaning *what* in Spanish,
or a mispronunciation
of *key*
locking me out
on the borders of infinity,
this space we call knowledge.

It's a reminder of a History lesson
back at school
something to do with King Arthur –
related somehow
but I'm not quite sure how,
as if history is a bundle
ever moving
tied in white. It's a veil
called kay,
a cloth, that Islamic word *ihram,*
symbolic of purity,
light as a word as a word could be.

But perhaps it is
a direct resonance
of an enquiry in Hindi or Punjabi
from a lover who says,
what do you want from me?
ki lene hai?
And there it stands,

dark and deadening,
calling a future gone by
like a dry hyacinth
pressed firmly in the pages
of a poetry book.

And deeper still
it's the instinctive sound,
the first utterance of a child
ka-ka
the moulding of speech,
a pattern or design being shaped.

Perhaps it's all four or five.
I don't know.
But it's more.

So I can't help seeing
beyond this figure,
this earth, our nature,
this clay that moves,
like radiance,
this key that fits
like melody in tune
drifting past the unknown,
mystical and mysterious
all the same.

And the way it stands abrupt and modest,
it could be a word
taken directly from the *Koran*
meaning love
or sacrifice.
Or *kaaba,*
that cube, the *Rosetta Stone*

fallen from the sky
the basis of human circumambulation.

It could be
Ka: that ancient Egyptian
spirit that dwells
like a vital force in man,
swooning the environment
like divinity
this thought we call reality.
And it collides
like autumn shades
this coil of complexity
moving into the distance
silently like the stars.

Kay for a poetic note,
Kay for legends,
Kay for spirits.

And still it persists,
this mass of moist solitude
forming metaphors in my head
of what, clay and key
and sound could mean,
could stand for.

And the eyes stare out, speaking,
nothing, nothing.
And everything.
I'm a little heaven on earth
built by Abraham,
this universe,
at a constant flux,
and beyond, and more.

Hearing the Notes of 'Fur Elise'

It'll be another new year
and what do you feel
a year older perhaps
maternal now
not so eternal
like Mother Earth
cold and polluted
cold and looted
serious not immaterial
what do you feel
what are your dreams
your wishes
your hopes
your expectations
for you and the world
for you and me
for snakes and rabbits
rats and dragons
are your thoughts alight
drifting gently
in your child's eye
through the spirit
of a *Diwali* night
are you holding onto your dreams?

What do you see
what do you hear
when the house is asleep
the silence hides
and the wind moves
in its listlessness
through commas

and short pauses
the slings and arrows
that separate us
irretrievably
Sita and Rama
in a Christian universe
can you see some hope in your dreams?

What do you hear
when the clock strikes twelve
and the Pole Star
sits in the East
harmonizing us
like the candles in a church
the notes of *Fur Elise*
you touch
the music of the hymns
or the sun
that woke the seeds
in water and clay?

Can you hear the past calling
a future dawning
love and forgiveness
hope and deliverance
over the rainbow
colours ignite
the angels delight
a peaceful world
silently
fading away
in the twilight skies
of pastures blue
and *Fur Elise* calling.

Ars Poetica

I wish I knew what a poetic-prose
was or is
and how it could be constructed
if construction it needs
in a post de-construction society.
I wish I knew its shape,
its form,
its language and syntax –
diction unique on its own and to me.
And if I knew,
I'd place you in the centre of the piece
like a sunset: you'd be the Word,
the soft alliteration,
the rhythmical chanting
of an unknown priest,
a superfluous echo,
quivering in a dusk-like dawn
filled with distance
in which I would see
the colours of our history,
like the robe of a maharaja,
a turban that sticks out in an English village
or a crown in the paddy fields
of the East.
In science you'd be the law of gravity,
the motion of the universe –
not quite alone
not quite comprehending,
fresh as a raindrop
falling like a crystal in the dark.
You'd be a love story
like *Romeo and Juliet*

or Sita and Rama
like *Antony and Cleopatra*,
the 'And' in the beginning of the *Bible*
or the colloquial innocence
of the last verse in *St. John*
portraying mysticism
like an ancient language
(Latin or Sanskrit),
romance and reason filtering
like a twentieth century thought,
a spirit of Sparticus or Cromwell
or Malcolm X.
You'd be the semblance of beauty,
a miracle on its own, a trick,
a mirage, a vodka with lime,
a Cuban cigar inhaled
softly and deep,
admired like the light in the Renaissance,
the unregarded genius like Ivor Gurney.
You'd be more than an elf,
more than life –
a spirit, a symbol of Time and Space
or the 'A' grade in an exam
like an encore
that means nothing and all.
At a deathbed, you'd be the last breath,
the climactic sound of loss,
that moment of parting,
the loosening of touch
like wonder and fear all rolled in one.
You'd be the poem that never was,
a subliminal metaphor,
an enigma
and this, me and you,
this thought about indefinability,

a prose piece not quite poetry,
moving stealthily in my mind
like a vision clearly reaching
but not, and never, quite you.

Co-existence

You live the moment purposefully.
I die just a little.

You call it summer, this sunshine that breathes.
I call it envy mutilated.

You call it tears, this volcanic eruption
Reaching high above the moon.
I call it silver spreading.

You sleep. I don't.

You call it a rainbow, this arch in the rain.
I call it design without meaning.

You see life, this thing you call love.
I see cold possibility.

Your look conveys clarity, a world of certainty.
Mine is a misused apostrophe
Occasionally colliding with your touch.

Cleaning our Silence

I can't remember when we first had sex
or thought of it. Was it in my pine-
wood flat in Nottingham during October or
was it in the backseat of your Cavalier
parked late at night on a double yellow
line off Broad Street, a fashionable spot
for distant lovers like us who prayed to
Guru Nanak or Krishna for forgiveness,
a day or two afterwards? Do you remember
sitting at the temple all so reverently in
pious clean silence, trying to focus on
the picture at the altar, at the *Granth Sahib*
and Guru Gobind Singh? Do you remember
it? And as you sat your face ashen
white with mourning I thought of your dirty
blue panties and clumsy white bra
that itched in the pouring rain outside.

We left ineffectually with an apple each:
talking softly, quietly with dreams.

Monastraki

(Athens, 1987)

We sat, depleted in the Grecian sun
a spruce tree shielded falteringly
a blaze in ninety degrees.

The Acropolis stood in the distance
like our pet dog, staring
indifference unconditionally.

You had a cup of continental coffee,
an espresso and some fresh salad:
I, a bottle of beer,

a *Heineken* and a couple of chilly
souvalkia, whose taste lingered
in my mouth (the meat raw on the spit)

when we arrived and parted silence
in the depth of the ancient metropolis.
In Omonia Square

people were prominent as a burning
hexagon to the bee. For an hour
and a half

we had walked through the blistering
heat of Junic Monastraki,
absorbing and eluding the Mediterranean

sun and rubbing our lingual deficiency.
And for a moment,
I was insidiously alert

to our cultural taste and feelings;
the peck on the cheek
a symbol

of the buried gulf between our powers
and our dreams – amidst
the sizzling waft of garlic

and ancient Greece.

'Thunder Road'

I pull in just after junction fourteen
on the M1, passing a light blue
'Welcome' service station sign.

The Sierra comes to a halt in front of me,
a silvery 1.8. I step out and
place the awkward nozzle

into the socket momently as I yawn
without covering my mouth
(my eyes blurry like the sunset

through the Sunday clouds). And I
watch the digits spin fastidiously, money
computerized. For a moment,

I'm aroused, the smell of petrol reminds me
of you, your Allegro and
sex in the backseat back in June '79.

The sky was an expanse of unromantic
grey above pastures red and blue.
You lay with your knees wide open:

the common position of a prostitute.
Our beat collided with *Thunder Road*
on local radio. And when you dressed,

I noticed my wet stain on your *shalwar*
hanging evidently indiscreetly underneath
your yellow *kameez* fashionably

designed in Southall. Your image
absurd and scattered like the fragrant
tissues, lying among the paper wrappers,

knocked off the dashboard –
a waft with a mixture of sweaty mascara,
leaky diesel and your garlic breath.

Watching 'Sholay'

I watch, I stare. It's midnight, quiet and strange.

Like a fungal infection it won't let me go
codified as a foreign film I picked up
at our local video store. I think I've seen
this curry western at least twenty times:
animated action juxtaposed with tacky dialogue –
overtly melodramatic, a fictitious piece too far-
fetched to link to reality, drama to my actuality.

I turn to the window to the comet, hovering
thousands of miles away, indecipherably.

Amitabh Bachchan's been shot over the bridge,
the bastard's dying – it's my favourite bit,
lyrically sentimental: moving and absurd simulta-
neously, a symbol of fallibility in a chaotic
      universe
denying a sense of structure or frame, yet
a symbol of India all the same.

Space: the lucidity of it all; the rocks hurtling;
the danger haunts me. Fear gripping, fear once
      more.

A song is played. Silence still: a conjunctive
      pause,
quite artistic.   It's a cultural oasis, the effects
of Americanization of the universe emblemised in
the coinage of Bollywood, through Regan's *Star
      Wars
Project*, NASA and *Space 1999*. And though I

     recognise
my Indian-ness (or is it because?), a deep rooted
repulsion escapes me, and makes me switch off
the video and turn to the pages of Friel and
     Wordsworth
to feel the illusion, the fabric of my world,
to feel the comforting Englishness (what was it that
Gandhi called us and Macaulay endorsed,
'the English-knowing men') that surrounds me, no
     irony
intended, merely words and wording, a constant
pretentious correctness in an environment
excluding undeniably.

And then I face the sky to observe the
     Constellation,
the delicate movement of the stars and the zodiac,
and feel a sense of losing in a cultural transit.

From the Somme to Donegal

A blue lily stem leant gregariously towards the
    conifers
at the back of our garden into a grenade of
    daffodils.

My son picked at it slowly tenderly like acid in a
    blood
clenched fist in Cromwell's *New Army*. Eventually
    he

ripped it apart shaking the morning dew on the
    trembling
gheeic grass, upon the salt-edged air wounded
    autumnally.

Seated inside, I gazed whilst sectarian news from
    Sky
echoed the Troubles and the Loyalist invasion of
    Donegal

and Amritsar – the old Orange Order executed
    separately
amongst a troop of tulips. The man said nothing of
    a temple,

gold and bullets, nothing of my uncle gunned to the
    ground
or his children who roam the town. And I thought
    of 1916,

Somme, concrete torn, revelling spades and guns
    throbbing

indiscriminately into force, a crackle of rifles, a
   wireless pause.

'I'm getting better, Dad,' he rejoiced running to
   me in hysterics
with a buttercup to his throat and I kissed him and
   smiled

momently as my eyes rove at the summit, a rump
   of clay
where lilies danced on our ashes, upon our grave.

Imperial Seminar
(The University of Nottingham, 1988)

'And that's it,' he concludes striding emphatically
　　into mid-air,
defining the absence of philosophy in the poetry of
　　Elizabeth Bishop.

The class sits, staring into silence, amplifying a
　　pause, eliciting illegibility
of an aesthetic thought.

No-one speaks. And then.

'There's a kind of strangeness, isn't there,' he
　　begins again rewording
the conclusion, *'this process of writing where the
　　individual is*
subtly, obliquely linked to the oppressed.'

'subtly, obliquely' echoes in my head like a distant
　　poem.

He waits, prompting a remark about Zibigniew
　　Herbert's unpunctuated speech
or Miroslav Hobub's pro-scientific clinical social
　　commentary.

But no-one speaks. For a moment.

Then Santosh, not quite on cue, formulates
　　restrained foreign intonation,
constraining to keep a strand of his syntax, his
　　Indian antiquity,
far too weak and falls almost into disarray.

The voice clashes
with the teacher's Irish protestation and perfection
    of academic expertise
whose independent word-patterns bombard like
    punctuation – indicative
of his superior knowledge, or lack of it.

And slowly Santosh retreats, colonized, while the
    teacher smiles.

Taj Mahal, Agra, 1650

And then, I notice how its marble arch
and minarets stand rocketing into the air,
a brilliant whiteness,

striking out into the distance
like nothing on earth,
a monumental reminder of human frailty,

where life lingers like hush and emptiness.
And it goes beyond space
and sleeping stars at night, this outline

against a cool, clear, deepening blue.
It's a scene unimaginable,
as if time stood still in these colours,

in this building, breathing such blue,
such white, whispering
something oddly close to love, and immortality.

Flash of Independence

We must at present do our best to form a class who may be interpreters between us and the millions whom we govern; a class of people, Indian in blood and colour, but English in taste, in opinions, in morals, and in intellect.
Thomas Babington Macaulay, Minute on Indian Education, 1835

We cram a photo booth at Digbeth
one Sunday afternoon in '89
waiting for the National Express.
We smile at Khalistan's Bhupendra Wala,
Bobby Sands and Blair Peach, indifferent
now to the violence and assimilation,
forgetting the rain outside, the clouds,
forgetting the fragility of our world,
the instability of our amphoteric lives
as British immigrants in an English universe –
while Gandhi weeps alone in the distance.

In a momentary flash we're a whole
a unit captured in time, not even
razor-sharp death can separate us.
Yet not a word or deed or countenance
can justify us completely. Like Mountbatten,
Macaulay's Union Jack and the scholarly
works on Shakespeare secure in the British Library,
we're a living irony detached and static,
moving like a spinning wheel of '47,
a symbol of India made in Lancashire –
while Gandhi weeps alone in the distance.

Abandonment

And I saw your car that night,
or a car that looked like yours, a dark Cavalier,
carcinogenic dark, near your house only a street
    away.
A black family owns it now. It must have been
    yours.
Did you sell it? Even the last three numbers,
worn-out grey, had a tint of familiarity.
Do you remember it? Back then, its engine would
    drone
like the breath of an asthmatic, our son, chronic –
desperately erratic. And often it would stop,
midstride, as if it was moving and dying
    simultaneously,
holding on for life, the outer limits of touch.
My body stopped, suddenly. I froze, like I'd seen
    you in person –
our case before history. And a heart that missed a
    beat,
flipped for acid, or oil to breathe.

Reading Heaney's 'The Follower'

It's that sound, the clicking of the tongue
not quite guttural, less wet than sharp,
a rasping sound I once heard or read

on a farm, appropriated like an order,
a piece of endearment, a suggestive
command: *'If you wouldn't mind, old*

chap.' It's an affectionate communiqué,
characteristic of an age of powerful politics,
a kind of wolf in sheep's clothing,

giving truth to a lie like India or Ireland –
permitting violence in degrees with
respectability (yes, respect, and yes, ability).

And it stays permanently in thoughts
and language, this offensive
which can last centuries. And, yes, it does.

Andromeda Falling

And there will be Time and Space
in our love
in our hopes of eternity.
And there will be tears for the young
untimely cut
Space and beauty encapsulated.
And there will be flowers softly laid
upon graves
full of broken dreams and promises.

The Crying Cats in Chandigarh

The air was thick last night
when I was terrorized
out of my sleep.

The meowing of the cats shot
through the silence.
Timmy was

there as well, tugging the pain
in unison
like the memories

you betray sleeping
a hundred miles away
in the next street.

You always said it was
a bad omen to hear
an animal cry at night.

I didn't think that nature
could be so real
to the nocturnal world

that swoons with the cats.
The moon was full and sharp
parading my conscience

as I pulled on the Venetian
blinds you bought from
Chesterfield.

It's funny, but once the air didn't
affect you like now
and your thoughts were

restrained, your rest
cushioned you like
a pillow sprinkled with

semen, blood and excrement
whilst my heart sat
wailing like the cats

in the next street
penetrating the reaches of our
past, moving

our history, our separate
being, closely,
like Le Corbusier's 1950s

sharing two states
betraying neither
completely.

Andromeda

If I slouch on a bus or a train in mid-afternoon
I can doze off for miles in time and half, detached

from a common-law wife, breeding madness,
    sifting silence
with a blade and an axe. I'm everything in one.

I can sing upon the highest tree, an oak, the furthest
mountain, the snowcapped peaks, transcending both
    time and form,

like a cosmonaut heading for space, climbing the
    rainbow
with a pulse or not, and the earth

pulling below or rising underneath his feet. I can
    lock,
steering the universe like Captain Kirk and his
    U.S.S. Enterprise:

'Steady as we go, Mr Sulu, steady as we go.'
The delicate positioning of speed and sound, I
    touch

like God, drifting deeper into darkness, that thicker
    space
eluding humanness and chance. And I feel this
    insignificance,

of being far and wide, passing East looking West,
and the stars, falling faintly behind.

On Viewing 'The Execution of
Lady Jane Grey'
(The National Gallery, London)

I'm reminded how phosphorous a piece of work it
    is,
how culturally Cretonnian in its texture,
faintly imperialistic, synonymous with wishing
    wells
and bluebells in a nine-day monsoon reign.

Its cinematic perspective, emotionally decipherized
brushed tightly in shades of red and black,
and the despair of the shadows clutching
the suffocating walls of 1554, closing in,

hold Delaroche to the Lady, unrealistic as she
is kneeling cushioned besides the crimson
gloom of the executioner and the staunch
blade of his axe, whilst the cut and the

cream of the nineteenth century dress radiates
the dry French straw. What words of
comfort must have been uttered by
the Constable of the Tower, what eyes, what

looks provided the impetus for this final scene
saintly canonized in this seventeen year
old queen, disturbingly serene yet
satanically pious and arousing to watch.

Eastern Thought-Reality

Achieving this takes five short steps in poetry:

One   Let's say we drink, slowly now, away from sports, TV sitcoms and chat shows, up to eleven, to the tolling of the bell and closing time, the shutting of doors, when night falls in the disquietude of our loneliness, our perfect imperfections, our hopes emptying, and us standing like spectators on the touch line, looking across a vast open space of *cushnai* and seeing nought.

Two   Let's say the world won't end today or tomorrow, that we don't have to have meaningless sex in a cheap motel, where the ambience is as outdated as the bed, hard and all, with curtains of floral designs from Laura Ashley, bleak and daunting, hanging like an unregarded metaphor safe in the distance, loitering with colours, dry as ashes, dead as the solemnity of a funeral procession, moving piercingly like a reminder that this, all, has no validity, this physical material world of metaphysics and reason, disintegrating, fading, falling in front of our very eyes, translates into nothing.

Three   Let's say that I've met history and made up with it, going back in time, surpassing Hinduism, and all the *isms* in our world, that she's forgiven me for having sinned this way or that, that I've made up with all the porcelain gods that govern us including the stars and position of the moon with the *Koran* and the *Gita* close beside me, illuminating like a lamp shade in the dark, ineffectually, standing just being, like herbal medicine without the side effects, like unconditional love or our one-night stand, back when time was everything and space was our school.

Four   Let's say we're spinning at sixty-five thousand miles an hour (and we are) like a ball out of control, dodging all the asteroids, all the rocks, but with a life of its own, probing on the depth of the universe, plunging into distant galaxies, revolving, turning upside down, in and out, drifting endlessly beyond the confines of our fear imaginings, calling logic and illogicality, going deeper than the permits of our cultural boundaries, daring, injecting images into our minds like railway tracks that open and converge, attracting and repelling far across space and distance, public and private simultaneously, all at once, like a *puja-room* sanctifying the household air mixed with joss-sticks and incense burners swirling around us like death and beauty, sparkling and speaking like the stars.

Five   Let's say that God doesn't care about who is who and what we've done or couldn't do – in fact, he doesn't exist – that she and I are still alone in separate worlds, untouched, defined by our conscience and faint memories, only our thoughts, our perpetual questioning of ourselves and what all this means, constantly binding us to paper, our dreams, our vision of life that wasn't quite there, our fear of death, our hopes of totality forming, flowing like this pen, like a birth, a voice, a heart beating softly, continuously, a rhythm, a metre magnifying, stressing the unstressable syllable, painting a meaning without the colours or the shades of our words, but rhythmical, always, like the chant of a village priest, healing, his echo bouncing off the shapes of the zodiac the cosmic order and, concentrated darkness quite unthreatening and....

voilà! – thought-reality.

The English Wallah

We're on an Avianca Boeing flight 702, ten thousand feet above the Atlantic Ocean. The Sirius is at my side, briefly, amidst a slight turbulence. I put down my copy of *Ulysses* on yesterday's *Telegraph*. The in-flight movie, *Beethoven*, flickers in front of me when I try to catch the eye of one of the Spanish stewardesses, and I notice my Aryan neighbour's whispering the paternoster in prosaic language, unlike the withered sepian Hindu woman a row behind me repeating Ram, Ram, Ram, in a rhythmical tone without fright or urgency, yet calm and soothing.

– *Ower, por favor.*

She smiles at my pidgin Spanish and I notice a slight gap in her upper front teeth. She looks so much like the woman I gave forty pounds to the previous night in Soho, where a Pathan friend took me after listening to Dr Johnson of Harvard lecture on 'The Political Allusions and Principles of Ancient Islam' at University College, near Euston Square.

– *Ah, you English, yes?* she replies in an awkward lingual familiarity. She's staring at my grey cotton shirt, collar unbuttoned, which Helen had bought from a shop wallah in Abadpur district of Jullundar the previous year, near the bus station where the southern local to Kartarpur terminates. I remember her phone call whilst the stewardess waits, slow motion. Freeze.

– *I'm quite close to your village. I presume you've heard Gandhi's been blown up. Poor bastard! And with a garland of flowers. Irony in motion – a theme for a poem, don't you think? We saw him in New Delhi only a few days ago... 'Got you something nice.*

I look up and notice her red lip-gloss, cheap and emphatic and it makes me want to kick her head in.

– *Sort of,* I shrug, cornering the American family looking sad and gloomy because Beethoven's dead.

'Sort of' reverberates for a second or two.

– *From?*

– *London.*

– *Ah, that's nice.*

– *Yes.*

– *You want water?*

– *Yeah,* I say revealing a fusion of identity.

She smiles a sultry smile and again I want to throw her on the floor and kick her head in, her accent and her looks. Punch her teeth out. Beethoven's a dog. He's alive, he's alive, you bitch! Instead I return her smile at her blue eyes and blonde hair. She walks away but her Chanel No 5 lingers in my mind and her nicotine-stained teeth survive like a snapshot.

I turn to the darkening window. It's late in the evening but I can still make out a stratum of cumulonimbus clouds lying underneath like candyfloss Uncle Ravi bought us in the summer of 1974 when I accidentally saw his Colt. 45 automatic safely tucked away in his glove compartment of his Ford Gran Torino.

– *Is it real?*

We were sightseeing in Los Angeles in an unglamorous part of Bel Air long before *The Rockford Files* and *Starsky and Hutch* hit our screens. We stopped to buy some ice cream at a drugstore with wooden carvings decorative as the colonial balconies in Plaza de Armas in Lima and just as civilising. A Mexican woman served us, her accent quite distinct, heavily foreign, and I noticed a trickle of perspiration under her armpits next to her prominent tits. There was a waft of tobacco, of cannabis, floating it seemed, unperturbed.

– *Gee it's hot,* she said. *But at least Nixon's gone, that lying son-of-a-bitch!*

The rest is a constant replay, a shot in the head, he's dead, he's dead. Just like Kennedy.

– *Fuck, look at the blood,* the blackman said, ganja smoke everywhere, part of my childhood haze and mystique.

– *Here's your water.*

The night was warm, intercepted with intermittent sounds of sirens of the ambulances and the occasional breeze when we parked in the hospital car park. A host of stars were out that night, like now, and I remember staring at the Northern Hemisphere, at the constellations, but I couldn't find the Big Dipper or the Bear. And in the corner of our universe, credits come up, the picture begins to fade.

The stewardess walks away and I can see the outline of her panties against her royal blue skirt, a dark sky and memories of Uncle Ravi and his words: **'Life's a quiet read, Son. Read slow.'**

No, I Am Not
Prince Hamlet

Self Indulgence

For spring, the break of the day, a bright dawn, for
my earliest memories, my nursery school, for my
toys, my *Action Man*, my cars, my stereotypes, the
formative point of my prejudice, for Miss Plant who
taught me nothing like Mr Cornick on the sports
field, where football and rugby were one, just
different sides of the same coin, for sci-fi, for the
rain-sodden Monday mornings, and the coldness of
it all, for *Starsky and Hutch* and television, for
George, my invisible friend who'll stay with me 'til
the end, for life outside books, outside poetry, for
day dreaming in the Science laboratory, for the cane,
the beatings, for being black and blue, and pale,
deep like the colours of my heart, for Mr Burnell
who taught R.E. with a Christian slant, for Maths,
for divisions and angles, for nought, for the weekly
spelling test, for our Head who betrayed us all, for
love and romance, for my first girlfriend, for the
mingling of blood back in April 1983, for idolising
her, for the scarcity of luck, for my son, who thinks
poetry sucks, for the work that I do and the air that I
breathe, for Beckett, Joyce and Hardy, for
universities and degrees, for my violation of
language, the few words I speak, for the dreams I
occasionally set, for my failures and successes, the
titles I never earned, the indisputable regrets, for my
parents' disappointment, their embarrassment, for
Hamlet, a teenage prodigy, my unrecognisable self,
my own tragedy, for the past, a time gone by, a life
that could have been, for dusk, for the starless night,
winter, the darkness of my age, this loneliness, this
window that translates the sorrows of my face, for

the distance from here to the edge of the world, for the first day of creation and Doomsday like the early morning crackle of Radio Four, Dogger to Malin, Finisterre and back again.

Santorini

I've still got that photo we took in Santorini
in that hotel we'd booked, white and bright
like heaven had descended on earth.

It was a day after you left your house in Peristeri
to elope with me, your English teacher
who thought you were pregnant.

I'm sorry if I gave you the wrong impression
but you meant nothing to me.
Like your name, that descended from Russia

you were never part of my dreams.
Emptiness stood before us
as we sat in the room with the large bay window,

its balcony beckoning us and voile curtains blowing
in the Mediterranean breeze.
Your *Kodak* automatic clicked

like a sign from the stars, an omen of some kind.
But you smiled on, obliviously. And me.
Neither of us knowing how we came to be.

Like that word *camera* which in Hindi,
also means *room*, your ancient Greek
and my antiquity embodied in one language.

So this photo we took back in '87 has crossed
two large continents, two ancient worlds,
two times. And still it mystifies me.

Winter 1972

We're in Maternity, Queen Elizabeth Hospital,
December 1972.

There's five minutes to go. But still no sound of
    parting
in this Ward 42.

My father sits in solemnity, dutifully; my mother
stares at the ceiling, glazed-eyes, burnt out,

and *Chitty Chitty Bang Bang*
mutely playing on a black and white screen.

It's a world of silence, the delicate descending
of a universe. Two worlds, two minds.

Pining to come, a minute to go. I look around.
This is a place where babies are born or die

like the falling of leaves, independent of our will
or choice or chance.

Outside the snow is descending in gentle abundance,
    softly,
Like the snow in Auschwitz or Passchendaele.

There's a bell, that passive lull, the sound of parting.
It could be a bugle call.

So we leave my mother – her eyes closed against
    this world:
one beat less; one mind less.

And when we come out, the moon is out with
    brilliance
and the snow is lily-blue,

smothering all that we call life and living,
and shrouding all that is dying and dead.

No Text From You

… There's nothing wrong with hoping is there?

The silence woke me last night –
that certain lull
of deadness
caught my ears
like an iambic beat,
its sound resonating
the covers of my sleep.
At the stroke of morn
it was,
when the world slept
(and you)
and the blank window
beckoned me
like an old school friend
I call *poetry*.

No text.

Outside, the sky stood tall
nothing stirred,
not a leaf, not a twig,
just the silence
that ancestral air
a slice of emptiness
piercing the silhouettes
loud and clear
like a painted wall,
in a forgotten dream.

Moonlight.

And you emerged from the dark –

your face and Teddy
our new born babe
(blotched and strewn as he is),
an image
I projected high
in a midnight sky
where millions of stars
and infinite galaxies
revolve and collide
instantaneously.

No text from you.

And you stand watching over me
like a constellation;
your name's a meditative word
the reverberation of *m*
shaped and defined by the *ah*
like some human consolation,
the *Mahabharat* defined
or that *pathos* captured
in a Greek tragedy.

Tonight, you're the *is*,
the temple on the Ganges,
that deep space
I haven't discovered
where *life* and *essence* emerge as one
folding you and me and hope,
not here
where time deceives,
eluding our thoughts
indifferently
like a godless being
or a benign benevolence

trying to conquer all
that we hope and imagine,
beyond this street where we live
strangely aware that this,
our flame,
means more than the fire of dawn.

And as I went to bed at three
I wondered if celestial bodies
also succumb to fate
and inevitability,
and stand as pawns
in the grand design of things
like you and me
like us
facing tomorrow briefly
this, you call *hope*
a microscopic dot
dulling out
in a hopeless universe.

And still no text from you.

Genista

*Marie: I want to live with you – anywhere – anywhere at all –
always – always.*
Yolland: 'Always'? What is that word – 'always'?
Brian Friel, Translations, 1981

It sounds like a bluey-mist of a star in another
    galaxy,
or a constellation discovered in Renaissance Italy.

Instead it's a Spanish plant, *genista,*
imported like Catholicism in the sixteenth century,
a metaphor for garden and politics.

And I remember my tutor who said that a poetic
    thought
must roll in your palm like an enigmatic seed
doling to breathe. Always.

My seed is this pen, these words that move
like some kind of life,
like something taking root upon this page.

And all this is strange
in the silence of this garden we shared,
where I sit with tulips and daffodils and marigolds –
a vision of your world, a picture of our yesterdays.

Today, I'm just a relic of a different century,
belonging to a different world.

How often have my thoughts eluded me
like dreams and my religious politics.
Like Time itself, or Space a million miles away,
difficult to capture in words.

But there's nothing to plant now, except definitions,
no choice but that insoluble mystery we call *destiny*:
perfection takes all.

And gazing across a random scent of colours,
our son clamours through the hawthorn bush –
an embodiment of that seed you'd sown
like *genista*, smiling like you. Always.

The earth, a Mediterranean lavender
and the sky, a Presbyterian blue.

Optical Illusion

Many a time my friend has explained.
But I still can't believe why it is that the sun

is bigger on the horizon than it is
when it's high in the sky.

Is it my eyes or the distance that deceives me?
If it's my eyes I should pluck them out,

if it's the distance space should engulf me.
A lifetime of sight and sound

has taught me nothing. Like an onlooker
who's been explained a simple card trick,

I still stand in awe each time.
And so, perhaps like Lear and Gloucester,

I should look at the world with my ears,
feelingly, for sound seems clearer

than our physical reality. (And in another
dimension, perhaps it is). But today,

I've given up my belief in something that isn't,
this vision I've kept, or a world not quite is.

Home-coming

It's late September back in '83. A cuculidean sky
stands hovering like death renewed.

My father takes my brother and myself to the
    Hockley
Flyover to show us a symbol of an era, his *des
    pardes.*

He tells us he remembers them laying the
    foundations
for this construction in the early sixties.

*It'll be the death of somebody this junction,
this traffic, this… someday.*

It's overcast as he talks viewing the scene carefully,
nostalgically, like an old school yard where he
    played.

He recalls the winter of 1963, the heavy snow
and the black ice that lingered on for weeks –

the dark coldness of those years are stained
in his memories like yesterday.

Naturally the random details flow: South Road,
Park Road, Benson Junior School… that's the pub

he and his mates used to drink in, *The Black Eagle*
on Factory Road, where James Watt built his engine

(or where they say he built his engine) and there's

the old fish and chip shop now an insurance office.

But the shops that housed a community have been
demolished, just the sixties tower blocks remain

and the graffiti slurred across time like *Pakis go
    home!*
(he tells us he always thinks of Bill Hayley's

Rock Around the Clock playing on the jukebox
when he sees that). And I can't help thinking of that
    world,

that harsh world when times were good and the gods
were smiling eternally. *But that was my plot,* he
    states

and stops as if trying to clear his thought, his vision.
Regrets, Dad? He shakes his head dismissively

into the void. *No,* he murmurs without a definition.
And all of a sudden he is silent as the rain begins to
    fall

descending through space like an estuary. It's the
    deep,
heavy rain, the biblical rain, the shedding of a
    galaxy,

piece by piece – star by star. And I notice his face
has changed somewhat: it's pale and hollow, his
    eyes

transfixed staring vacantly, like Lazarus returning
from the tomb, dead for days or was it for weeks?

It doesn't say. But for an instant, it's like the end
of the world, a dark malignant cloud teases him,

a reminder that death is forever permanent,
that concrete half in our consciousness.

Within seconds the moment passes and we turn to
    go.
But on our way back, no-one says a word,

just the silence speaks like a bad omen.
As if his *maan* had seen his own funeral.

Meeting Hitler

What, though better unsaid would we have history say
Of us who walked in our sleep...
Louis MacNeice, Epitaph for Liberal Poets

I've read that Nazis were looking for
the gene that causes ageing. Say if they had.

The implication of it keeps me awake occasionally.
Today, I shudder to think of the possible reality,

for everything that is would not have been,
and everything we imagine, just history.

What if Hitler or Mussolini had found it,
would they have abandoned the quest for
    knowledge,

or the search for the *Holy Grail*?
Six million Jews for Eternity – an ace up their
    sleeve.

And what of our sense of horror
substituted and obliterated with snippets or cyanide

flashing above Europe like shooting stars
or space satellites.

And Chamberlain's Munich speech
echoing youth and vibrancy recorded on appease of
    paper

so pure, so green, so terribly English –
call it *imperialism, racial purity* or *ethnic cleansing,*

as if *difference* is just a word called MacNeice.
and words can make a difference, instantly.

Re-discovering 'King Lear'

Claire found it in her school cupboard, Colin says
    leaning forward,
passing it to me like an old piece of education.
It's the New Clarendon Shakespeare's edition of
    King Lear

edited by Ralphe E. C. Houghton M.A.
Formerly Fellow and Tutor of St. Peter's College,
    Oxford.
Published by the Oxford University Press, 1957,

it's been reprinted several times over concluding in
    1978
for my untraceable universe, my comprehensive
    school
and me. *Strange how it got there*, he ponders
    vaguely

crossing into another metropolitan borough –
    Stoke of all places!
There's a pause as he fumbles back into his chair.
Your name's on the inside cover, he states pleased
    with himself

as if clenching a deal, a sale he's made. In my
    hands, I sense
an old familiarity that passes through me like *déjà*
    vu.
It's royal blue, antiquated a little, on the trailing
    edge of an empire,

smudged through the parchment on the left hand

corner,
and yes, my name's there, printed clearly in blue.
    The *R*'s looped,
rather uncertainly, a remnant of a grammarian
    influence,

not the *R* I use today – a zorro slash intercepted
    urgently
with a lower case *L* conveying the re-enforcement of
    a dual-identity.
Back then *dual* and *identity* weren't cajoled into a
    compound word.

Back then they stood apart, distinctly, separately
    like Toby
who was always picked last on the sports field at
    Metcheley Lane.
And it's odd how after twenty-one years not a trace
    of me remains.

All my notes have been rubbed away, replaced with
    a new language,
a new identity. My book, my name is merely a
    commodity
to use over and over again for the sound editorial
    wisdom

of Ralphe E. C. Houghton M.A. that emblem of an
    age
shrivelled like me at the finishing line of History,
    captured
like a philosophical idea, call it *literature* or
    settlement.

And I think of Roman roads and Egyptian tombs

neither here nor there – not dead nor living, just
   being,
breathing time and space as if they're one and the
   same thing.

Falling Star

You called me late at night mid-December
to tell me your father was dying in a cold foreign
   bed
at a hospital in Athens.

Forgive me, my love, I was only half awake
but I heard your recognitioning –
your soft despair at a darkened sky
where morning was a thousand miles away.
I heard the cold comforts far from home –
the ancient tones of Monastraki
stretching out from here to Sophicles
from your world to mine
intersected somewhere by language.

And I heard you describe his face, that point
of awakening, that hollowness, the acceptance of
   grief.
In a second, it was purity you saw, quietly,
like a line from a hymn, *like the birth of a child,*
that first breath, deep, bright and beautiful.

You sobbed through the phone
passing thoughts from a different universe
where gods excelled and no-one cared a bit.
Not a word, not a sound could have pulled you away
from the mire of a fallen star you called Thanasus
through which life rose and died
amidst the flicker and the glitzy-glitter
of our Christmas tree.

Difference

You don't really sense *difference*
that you're someone else,
in fact, you become multi-faceted,
you're an actor, say,
strutting and fretting
playing many parts,
to borrow a bastardised phrase
from the bard of all bards,
but sometimes the notion,
that thing called *difference*,
bursts in front of you
like something falling from the sky,
like a piece of a meteorite
Muslims believe to be from God,
the sacred rock,
the subject of their pilgrimage,
the basis of *haj*,
enough to excite Richard the Lionheart
kept him abroad
much of his life.
Take that time I was in Amritsar,
at Jal'ean Wala Baag
looking at the bullet holes
of the British guns
when, our guide,
a dark, gangly man,
tells us thousands of Indians
lost their lives –
but in actual fact,
only three hundred and fifty,
Peter Rhodes,
a distant Jew familiar

with the receiving end of atrocities,
corrects me
when I quote this as a *fact*,
ingeniously through the e-mail,
on my return to Britain,
as if facts *are* facts
and can't be distorted
like the six million Jews whose fate
lay in the hands of SS generals.
The guide smiles
emphatically,
pointing to me and my son,
joking, (tongue in cheek?)
It was you English, who did this!
At which point
an awkward silence emerged
and a line from Eliot's,
The Burial of the Dead:
Bin gar keine Russin, stamm' aus Litauen,
echt deutsch
echoed in my head.
And, bumph!
There it was
that difference captured
for posterity like a snapshot.
My son and I stood bemused
staring at each other absurdly
as if it was
a truth only half spoken
what us? English?
'Couldn't help feeling lost
being there
but feeling here
and vice versa
as if roots are something

you carry with you
like money or visa cards.
Perhaps nothing is quite
as it's spoken,
or appears as it is.
As Hamlet said,
there are more things
in Heaven and earth
than dreamt of
in your philosophy books.
Indeed.
And I suspect that,
maybe just a weeny bit,
that also applies
to poetry and prose
no matter whatever literary tradition
you're developing
or emulating
no matter whatever form or shape
you might want to think.

Miss Plant

Ophelia: *Good night, ladies, good night. Sweet ladies, good night, good night.*
Hamlet, Act IV. Sc. V

I Scene

She was petite and angelic
back in my fifth form in 1979,
rather like a dandelion, delicate to the end.
Soft she was like Ophelia,
a line in monosyllabic words
perfected by a poet,
just couldn't go wrong.
And often in her class,
I'd imagine that she was a wave
blown in time that rhythmical,
senseless thing –
a pattern of life and death.
Nothing hindered her; nothing touched her.
She was that frail serenity,
that close-up, a focus of flimsy mind…

II Life

One. Stop. Two. There now, ninety degrees.

Her Yorkshire vowels echoed through the class,
along the corridor, loud and silent,
perfect and dead,
the playground battlefield –
the violent retreats of an unfettered mind.

III Equation

Her words swayed
like psychedelic music
translated into arithmetic
as if perfection can be measured in angles
and translated into definable forms
of rhythmical speech...

Eighty degrees. Even Maths can be emotive, you
  know,
Rosh, like your poetry.

IV Death

Then. It was a sky-lit morning in June
during assembly
when Mr. Cunningham,
a head teacher far too tall,
standing heroic and glum,
told us an irony of all ironies
that she'd passed away.
Quietly, he added
as if life is a transition
between stages of regression
defining what we are and what's to come
whilst cancer hung in the air
like a dirty word.

V Mourning

Two weeks later, before school,
Jennifer took her petals
and peonies
crying as she laid them
on her grave,
that shady spot at St. Mary's Church
where nothing grows
and soil is dead
as barren earth of centuries ago.

I stood at the gate with my copy of *Shoot* –
Man. United had lost to Liverpool or Coventry
and Joe Jordan had been sent off again.

VI Puzzle

The grass was wet with dew and a deftly silence
submerged us like a different world.

VII Aftermath

And for a moment, I felt the absurdity of life
as I looked at the grave, like a false equation,
something indefinably gone wrong,
a symbol intact,
like mutability,
that illusory world cemented,
six feet under,

though herself only five feet four.

Doha

Your talk about *lehenga* designs
was an anointment

like a special *arti* or *pooja*.
I saw your eyes light up

like Persian silk,
as you pulsed about

the latest style
in shalwar-kameez,

imported in the *Bindya Collection*
you had seen in the high street.

Forgive me, my sweet,
but I wasn't listening.

Instead I was suspended
quite deep

between memories of your illness –
that night,

your legs sprawled across
your bathroom

as you vomited –
and of how soft and small

your breasts were
when we lay together

for the very first time.
And tonight,

with your eyes transfixed
on Doha, you say

This is just a wank,
summing it up

defining the inevitable
conclusion

where, alone
you're adamantly

insisting, we're
headlessly heading nowhere.

Readiness Is All

It's not that I'm losing it
or anything
but ever so often –
or at least occurrences
at definite intervals,
more now than ever before –
especially late at night
in the midst of a darkening sky,
I kind of sense
that note of Hughes,
that poetic depiction
that *something else is alive*
beside the clock's loneliness
and I don't mean the muse,
but the calling of life
a resonance, a tone
outside this world,
or something moving
between the rustle of the leaves,
at the rhythm of the heart
tick, tick, tick
a reminder perhaps
a record of writing and thought
of old age
like that time when Uncle Ravi
slipped away
with a bullet through his lungs
I sensed it then
that movement,
the ebbing away of life
and something intrinsically
grave and hollow

like the opening
of *Moonlight Sonata*
slow, cold and morbid.
I can't play this, said
the Countess Guiletta,
the object of Beethoven's love,
It's like a funeral piece.
It may be, but still
it reaches out
and touches the very soul
of man, by which, of course,
I also mean woman.
So perhaps my tutor
was right when he wrote
how the ear
was the only true reader
registering the minuscule
beauty of verse
the rest was merely *a turd shrine*
I call my personal wisdom
where life and sound
are all very relative,
everything is
(dictated by Darwin's theory)
largely ephemeral
one thing giving way
to another
where nothing's so sanctimonious
or conclusive
as religious beliefs,
at which point, for a moment,
I try and recall
what Hamlet said,
resigning to the complexity
of life and being

embracing the special providence
in the fall of a sparrow,
that philosophical
afterthought, which,
like the ramblings of a well-meaning poet,
may or may not
be bullshit,
now what was that he said
about readiness is all?

No, I Am Not Prince Hamlet

No, I am not Prince Hamlet
that turd of a scholar
that spoilt brat
a pseudo-dramatist
if ever there was one
a wife batterer
and a psychopath
a mere utterance
of Anthony or Coriolanus
or the brief candle
that Scottish king
Macbeth
the non-committal *Amen* man.

Maybe I could pass for
Edmund
the bastard
the base of all bases
the Machiavellian one
but not Hamlet
who I wouldn't want to be.

I'd rather be Richard the Second
the poetic crown
that ineffectual
and disastrous king
or even Richard the Third
the hunchback
the murdering unc
the villain of all villainy.
Not Hamlet
the self-conscious one

not a scholar nor a king.

I could be Falstaff though
with all the drinking I do
my cowardice
and suspicions
my protruding paunch.

Certainly not Prince Hamlet.

Othello perhaps
his startling stupidity
his many faults
his jealousies
the obsession
with possessions
the instruments of his plague
or even Iago
on certain nights –
my conscience
getting the better of me.

Not Hamlet.

But maybe Oswald
the obsequious lord
verging on getting it
from his mistress
or Polonius
the fumbling, rambling
arse
the oily art of politics
high and mighty
a shadow
in the face of Hamlet.

Maybe I could pass
for the Earl of Warwick,
the Kingmaker,
the attendant lord
or Rosencrantz and Guildernstern
or Valdamir and Estragon
struggling to find
where they are
and what it all means
looking for a point
in the plot
that language
they use
their identity flowing
into one another
while the seal they carry
the meaning of life
seals it all.

But never Hamlet.

The Notes of the Rani
*Upon Watching **The Royal Family**, 1969*

I was seven when I saw you on a black and white
   screen
A time when the world was a mysterious commodity

Unique and obscure like *The Rain-Charm for the
   Duchy.*
That doleful dignity stood defiantly like John the
   Baptist,

Gracefully like perfect stillness, perfectly.
That language echoed clarity and antiquity

Like the clear sharp outline of a midnight moon,
Smiling upon the Crown like pomp and majesty.

Oceans can rise in leaps and bounds, they say,
Like a lyrical sonnet piercing the heart.

Perhaps they can. Back then that voice was a
   youthful
Harp or a sitar faintly playing, falling like the stars.

But it wasn't your English consonants clashing
With my foreign vowels that touched me then,

Or the structured restraints of dangling chords
That appealed to my senses. Instead,

It was that deep resonance, that rare presence
Of a different world hanging like a poem in my
   class.

There was that voice out of my touch, in another
	league,
Like the man on the moon, magnetic as the *Rosetta
	Stone*

Or Kaaba in the East, filtering through time
Like *ambiguity* invading my culture and youth.

And I remember Armstrong's animated prose
One small step... washing over the unease of
	Annenberg's

Fumbling *refurbishment, rehabilitation.* So tonight,
I see age as a linguistic thought, the grouping

Of words and intonation that touches the state
Of *nirvana* where your eyes still dance like a
	haunting,

The omniscient guide, in a turbulent universe.
And amidst a Plantagenet sky, softly speaking still,

I think of Annenberg and Armstrong and Hughes,
And the flights and flutterings of your words

Descending like Christmas rain, like *holi* confetti,
Deep in motion. As if you're probing the past

Patiently, like an advocate of the English law.
For this is what you are and all that we stand for.

A Wish for Tomorrow
(For Holocaust Memorial Day, 27th January 2001)

Above this bridge, a dove is flying high in the sky
Into the northern constellation

So clear at first and then a distant blur that only
   Time
Can bring.

I wish, I wish...

Underneath, the neon lights of the cars whiz pass,
Vans, lorries and trucks –

The remnants of life in motion, with all our
   corrections
And gross imperfections.

I wish... upon a star...

Instantly, I can't help thinking
Of ethnic cleansing or concentration camps,

How the spirit of man is challenged at every corner,
At every stop, at every age.

I wish upon a star tonight...

So here in this dark, Dresden, Auschwitz
And Belsen stand not so much like failures

But foundations of the human spirit,
Striding ahead, valiantly,

Mapping the brave new world which millions didn't
see.
And there's hope for the world, still,

This star we call home
Where all our forget-me-nots are tucked away like
dreams.

I wish upon a star tonight,
Twinkling high above...

And though I live in the past, I believe in the world -
All our tomorrows, like that flying dove.

And as I watch the sky tonight,
I wish, I wish you love.

The Central Library

(The Central Library) is like a place where books are incinerated.
HRH Prince of Wales, BBC, Omnibus, May 1988

I've read that you're coming down,
marking the end of an age, the passing of time.

You stood tall throughout my youth
you, my O'level days of the seventies
you, my hideaway, my secret den
my literary construct –
a child of the sixties.

In the eighties,
you played Reason in a turbulent universe
you, that was serene and quiet
the cultural oasis of contemplation
the modest intellect
fading away like a monastery –
and their burning of books outside your door.

In the nineties,
you played the role of my reference,
my bearing, my guardian,
a poem in the making,
you that *life* in a dying world
a blighted star
the focal point of protests and demos –
skateboarders and refugees.

In history you'd be the republican, the genius
the constitutional architect
the formulator of democracy,
or a document like the Magna Carta

139

or the Bill of Rights –
the thorn in the side of royalty.

You acted as a symbol, like a discerning belief
a sacred place, holy as the Vatican
or the Ganges
prominent as the Chinese Wall
and just as deep –
where God was dissected like a museum piece.

You were the *thought*,
a microcosm of my world
you, who were rich and rare,
a statement of Time personified
not the past or the present –
but a picture of tomorrow that never was
like the unforeseeable wine bars and *McDonalds*
that emerged like cancer growing inside you.

And perhaps, today,
you were not so much a failure
but an incomplete hope in a jaundiced world
of money, aesthetics and government policies,
crumbling away like a meteorite
or an asteroid heading for earth,
a revelation defined by a scientific law.

And so you're coming down,
book by book at the turn of the century
rejuvenating in another world
marking the passage of Time –

taking rubble to rubble, dust to dust
and, with it, all my ashes.

Descartian Thought

It's that moment that lies between the sliding
of the doors and the movement of the tram –

that certain hum and a drone of the engine,
that makes me wonder about the state
of my own sanity.

I swear, doc, that sometimes,
I don't know if I'm a man dreaming he's a poet
or a poet who thinks he's a tram.

Walking Amongst the Trees

We read that night after night there were air raids
Like the demented hooting of an owl during 1971 –

An echo of the unsettled conflict, that tearing apart
Of Kashmir. Do you remember it?

I could have been there in the Muslim village of
    Rahimpur
Or in Britain of 1942. No difference really.

Were you writing *Khadi Boli* then or planning your
    radical
Shake up in Delhi? Perhaps you weren't.

But life continued here in our back yard quietly –
Like another world, fish and chips and a second-
    hand T.V.

Then. A misty morn in November that year,
The kind you might have seen on your walks in
    Manali.

An Urdu air-mail letter arrived here in London.
Quietly my father opened it.

Elders of the village had advised my uncle
To have our house repainted a dull morbidness.

White reflected too much light in the dark, he wrote.
Too dangerous. We'll be lit like a spotlight.

My father glanced at the *Des Pardes*, lying open

Like a revelation, a Sikh intermediary,

Whilst Krishna and Mata Shere'an Wali stared out
From the crowded mantelpiece.

I hope you won't mind, my uncle concluded.
Of course not, my father replied, *paint it.*

Within days he did, a murky orange
Like the third of a new found flag standing in the
    sunset

Side of our village, the colour that led you on
In the political scene.

Then one night I had a dream that I came home
From school one afternoon, my friend and I,

Pausing in the shade of a grandfather tree, *Baapji* –
Presiding over a well of cool possibilities

That lay beneath us. Suddenly, the sharp mournful
Drone of an engine, then a thud of lightning

In the cornfield, fully ablaze with future atrocities.
An enemy pilot shot down

In the afternoon sun – the days of Emergency.
Everyone rushed out. A cacophony of sound

And movement amidst the blurring of time and
    distance.
And even though I didn't know you, still a belief

That one day that Land of the Five Rivers

Might rid itself of tyranny, the infamous dynasty.

For years my father and his brothers waited,
Not for a mythological figure but a Sanskrit pandit,

Plainly speaking from the mountains of Manali to
   Agra,
From Kashmir to the walls of Delhi.

Words fell like raindrops from an August sky
Softly falling on your premiership in '98.

So was that you back then walking amongst
The untouchable calm, of the Manali scene,

Thinking deep, this notable territory Kashmir.
And did you hear the longevity of the Indian trees?

Millennium Christmas

A gentle rain falls through the universe now
Not snowflakes on this Christmas Eve –

A trickle that shimmers like diamonds
Against our Nordic galaxy.

All around, the stars glimmer, these words,
Like omniscience that see all –

Eluding the hands of fate like beings
Of a different world.

Amidst the darkness of this Space
Wet-silence seeps into our thoughts

Like the flickering flame of a diva,
Or the hush of hymns in a church.

And this could be an insoluble instance,
Or an enigma for the essence of earth,

Projecting a collision of sparkling rain
With an image of that Child's birth.

Facial Definition

My elderly barber, Hanif, often boasts
about having met Elvis outside Madison Square
   Garden
on a bleak afternoon in 1972

(has a black and white photo to prove it –
somewhere).

He's also met Mohammed Ali, a day before
his fight with Joe Frasier back in January 1974.

Quite worldly is Hanif.

Today he claims he can tell the difference
between a Kashmiri Muslim and a Hindu.
It's all in the face, he says finishing off
my short, back and sides and handing me a tissue.
Look at this one walking in. Definitely a Hindu.

Are you a Hindu, Asif? I ask my friend
for confirmation as he takes off his coat.

Fuck off, Rosh! he retorts sharply (it's Ramadan).
A waft of a cockney accent resonates
cutting through Elvis playing on the CD.

And I glimpse at the mirror: Hanif, bare-faced,
sweeping the hair away,
while Asif takes a seat, smiling discretely.

Omen

A cancerous cloud hangs
over me ominously

dark, dank and deep,
the colour of a smoker's lungs.

It's a like a sign
of the monsoon

as I leave Gloucestershire
on a sodden Tuesday afternoon.

There's a crackle of a dial
in this promise of the rain,

whistling imminently,
like mourning

of some kind.
And I hear it again

this word, *terrorism*
that terrorizes me.

My car stands alone
in the space I left it

obediently like a pet dog
soldiering to guide me out

like a strident foreign policy
or the way people

take God for reality
The key turns

under the darkness
that looms above me,

obnoxiously.
And then, slowly

I move off
amidst a sudden barrage

of hailstones,
an onslaught of arrows

showering
the Tewkesbury battlefield,

a twirl of chaos
in this place

of kings, queens
and castles,

the remnants of the Crusades.
Not suicidal bombing

I'm hearing on the radio.
And it persists,

this absurdity
on the World Trade Centre

and the Pentagon.
Driving up on the M5,

it's hailstones and lightning
for some miles

the rain seeping
through my head

like the fight of the Roses
or the Hundred Year War,

an echo of history
like Pearl Harbour

breaking through
the weather forecast

on a foreign radio station
but it's all Latin to me,

or Greek, or Arabic.
Not New York.

Not today
when people are

rubble and dust
and buildings

blown away
like ashes.

Oh, Time, upon
whose hands

we dream of heaven,
guide us out

into your shelter, out of this hole,
this so dark, this so deep.

The Delicate Falling
of a God

I

I was driving home that day from Gloucestershire –
had just hit the M5 at Bristol trying to keep an eye
on the road ahead, the traffic, and wiping away
raindrops in a clear blue sky which were falling
upon the cacophony of twenty-first century
Christendom. I had been recording something or
other at the BBC on Whiteladies Road near Black
Boy Hill, had had lunch near the suspension bridge
overlooking the mammoth ridge etched above a
gateway to the underworld or not, of history, poetry
and the BBC.

And as I made my way onto the motorway, it
seems incredible to me now that I was inert and
oblivious to all that was about to unfold around me,
preoccupied by my own performance at the studio,
as if I were the centre of the universe, that the stars
stood for me like spotlights and that I could control
them at will, by acting, by moving on a stage as if
my chance and its coming round is my choice,
determined by me and me alone.

And in that self-satisfied state, hedonistic turmoil, I
flittered from one thought to another, rather like an
undefined consciousness, a trail that was leading to
nowhere but to myself.

Abruptly the news flash on the radio, tangled words
about New York, a plane and the World Trade
Centre. Suddenly the clouds gathered around me
like an omen of some kind, a prowling beast
moving towards me. And then within a distance of
no more than ten miles, there's repetition, another

plane, and *terrorism* breaks out, a word more deadly than ever before as if touching my world for the first time and Islamic fundamentalists standing in a surreal panoramic vision.

All of a sudden it wasn't the Middle East then, but New York as if, for the first time, our realities were really colliding.

They say that sometimes you can glimpse or feel a future you didn't plan or see. At that moment, I saw something unholy, as if history had come and gone and had left no distinguishing mark or impression on our perception of reason or logic. It was all dry and useless, unperturbed like soot that had built up over hundreds of years.

And I remember looking up and sensing the sky standing motionless, the world not breathing, as if hearing the next stage in the movement of the universe. And I had this inexplicable urge to speak on the mobile phone, to listen for comfort. All I wanted was to hear your voice, a simple utterance of familiarity because for years we had lived without living, merely existing as extras waiting at the wings of a grand stage. In your voice I knew I'd be able to feel a sense of now, self and place. But nothing came.

In seconds, like the turning of a leaf, I watched the looming battle of the gods and ideologies, and the world dividing. The arena set for a grand finale.

II

A vertical construct
is a skyscraper,
each block a frame
of our lives,
our security.
And when it crumbles
through a belief –
or half-belief –
I see Man
as a dream,
quiet and frail,
like the delicate falling
of a god.

VII

Just think
all this

one day
all this

fading
into thin air

not a stone
or a brick

in sight
not a tear

nor a word
just think

all this
all of it

ascending
with the rising dust

only your look
our children

and these words
remaining

forever
like evidence

of a dying
world

that's crumbling
like a relic

of a bygone age
or language

(Latin or Sanskrit)
that ceases to be,

or gets distorted
by history

id est the way
Himmler

(with the aid
of Ernst Schäfer)

linked lingual
patterns

for his own
grand purpose –

that theory,
the survival of

the fittest gone
mad.

For *ayran*
read *arya*.

Yes, we're
talking

about extinction,
dear.

Let me say it again
x-tink-shun.

IX

If your book is full of words
give me a word

to soothe away
all my hopes

of yesterdays.
Give me a word

that explains
what I see

what this means,
where God is

if God *is* at all,
blessing this

this mass of chaos
unfolding.

Give me a word
to help me see

beyond all this,
beyond this world

flickering in time
like a funeral pyre

and everything,
all our follies,

swarming around
like cells

in the vessels
of the universe,

the dark frozen
depths

of our blighted
souls

which some say
speak to us

in the obscure
deadness of the night,

that *midnight
moment's forest*

when language
penetrates

all our awakenings
Gas, Gas, Quick boys!

from the classroom
to the field;

from the obscurity
of science

to the long power
of poetry.

X

Who said, *do not go gentle into the good night?*
That's just poetry.

All around it's rage I see
rage, rage, rage.

But thoughts of you gentles me
just a little

when the rain falls and sun shines
like memories of all we are

a Sunni Muslim, a crazed Shiite
or an emerging shibboleth.

And though *the light has gone
out of our lives*

and darkness is everywhere
I will use

the only arms of defence:
silence, exile and cunning

like a torch in a forest
full of death and mosquitoes.

And the faint echo of your breathing
touches me

like joss-stick scent
In a dark *puja-room*,

full of secret hopes
in a dying world.

XI

I'll weigh these words
in the palm of my hand

to see what they are
and how this fits in

with everything I know
of education.

Guide me out of this,
you stars

because my god
is falling from the sky

landing between *jihad*
and the *crusades*

where philosophy
doesn't exist

and human beings
paint themselves like you

delving deep
a million miles in space

where no-one speaks
and an echo

drifts, like a surreal
dream –

a backdrop (the outline)
in a film or a play,

a stinking stench
of deadness, decay or fish.

XVI
(For Anjana)

Quietly we play building this tower
to the sky.

Your face, a picture of careful
concentration.

You place your blocks gently,
softly like innocence

on wafer-thin ground
whilst clutching my hand for guidance.

Your contorted smile,
your deftly silence.

And then at last, you rise
like a whispered prayer,

tiptoeing across the floor –
hoping the tower won't fall.

XVIII

We sit ominously
soft and aimless

for the ticket machine
to get to seventy-seven

when my father's turn
will come up

like an awakening
in the dark,

and a needle will puncture
a cold extraction

of red, the linkage
of life and lineage.

And in that moment
that body will snap

a sample from
two thirds of water

to be placed like a drug
under the microscopic eye

of medicine or language
that records our life

slow as a timepiece
in the A & E.

And then a heartbeat,
a movement

a reminder of our cold
existence,

our hopes, our thoughts
and all we are

thumping down
like a sentence decreed

by an English judge
in an English court

where fate loiters
in the corridors of uncertainty.

XX

There is a land of the living and a land of the dead, and the bridge is love.
Tony Blair quoting Thorton Wilder on 20th September 2001
at the memorial service in New York

Do you remember when we first kissed
or that time when I told you

I love you?
That moment so rare, so light

you thought I'd forgotten it,
didn't you?

A couple of years before
we'd sat at the Crown and Angel

at the corner of St. Martin's Lane
and New Row

(near Covent Garden)
in a state of giddy-stupor

and then wandered around
the National Gallery.

You laughed uncontrollably
at 'The Execution of Lady Jane Grey'

when I had said,
'It's forever in my mind.'

You were loud like a schoolgirl
on an outing

'Forever?' you repeated
in your Lancashire drawl,

'What do you mean, *forever*?'
and giggled teasingly –

your rosy cheeks, your freckles
and red hair.

I'm at that point now on the edge
of that word *forever* and I'm about

to see the fabrics of this world
and this thing we call *finality,*

like the taking of the seed of life,
our choice. My heart has grown,

like the spirit of Lady Jane Grey.
And as I fall, all around

I see the fading away of light,
the lifting of a *burka* –

the clarity of an illusion –
where water glides

like a paper plane carrying
our hopes, a sense

of *otherness*. And in that airiness,
that lightness of blue,

is a bold link, call it *love,*
that bridge we've built,

between the living and the dead
like that painting hanging

violently in the Gallery
conveying some romanticized

vision of *Englishness* –
not abstract but divine actuality.

XXIII

The cradle rocks above an abyss...
Vladmir Nabokov, Speak, Memory, 1951

Everyday I felt I was falling into the abyss
of neurosis not knowing how or why
I came to be who I was.

And then I saw you and we talked
the night before I heard the news on the radio
that the world was crumbling to bits.

And I described you as a huddling old hag,
your face falling apart loosening like a rubbery
thing. You cried, I remember.

And then we lay silent for much of the night.
Even dawn appeared like *a brief crack of light
between two eternities of darkness.*

It's the taking away of you from me
from life and history, like perfection
as if the light had revealed all.

And not all my apologies could save you
from the graveyard of our relationship
where truth should never be acknowledged.

XXVI

...you have to believe God has a plan.
Rudolph Giulian, Mayor of New York, 2001

Occasionally in our lives, once in while, we come
across a whirlwind from our cold frailties that
speaks and shocks and reminds us of who we really
are – not the kangaroo court we're in.

So smear your face and nose,
butter your finger nail,
bless your friend and foe,
this world it has to fail.

And then it vanishes into thin air like confetti on
Flag Day – the stuff of kind democracy, a glossy
gathering, a stream of pageantry, lords and ladies,
kings and queens, gods and all. But it's an illusion
unobtainable like timelessness and infinity.

So shape it as it's falling,
point an iron rod,
hear your conscience calling,
and never speak of God.

XXVII

'Home'? What is that word 'Home'?
Richard Bach, There's No Such Place as Far Away, 1977

This is where your guru stood
your inspiration,
at the end this cobblestone alley –
when he gave you a glimpse
of your future world, my world.

You were only six or seven
that night when you saw Him –
a beam of light had lit his head
whilst you played hide and seek
or its equivalent in a Punjabi universe.

And this, my prayer is just a prayer
not unique or personified *dis*belief,
not the finding of a god or my home,
in this your alleyway.

I've merely come to pay my respects,
to you and your guru, to your village,
to your array of stories
which I believe or half believe –

not knowing quite how or why
we've never quite fitted in,
not in the idolised past you've built
or Britain in your dying world.

XXIX

A photograph...is a trace, something directly stencilled off the
real, like a footprint or a death mask.
Susan Sontag, New York Review of Books, 23rd June 1977

Nothing stays the same
not as it is
not as it was

as if our disasters
are reminders
of our vulnerability

when they touch
our perceptions
of ourselves –

like photographs –
that stick
in the memory bank

and tug at the cold frailty
of our lives
as if the universe

will engulf us,
swallow us up
in its timeless bang

the distant hollowness
of space –
traced off or erased

like indecipherable reality,
a cheap animation

something close to foreign

like a footprint of life
quietly subdued
serene as an old man

draped in a *doti*
in the early Indian morn.
And all standing still.

XXX

...the sunset would deepen through cinnamon to aubergine
Paul Muldoon, Gathering Mushrooms, 1983

'The world is an oyster,' they say,
though to be honest,
it's more like turmeric *keema*
cooked on a clay oven in the midday heat,
where the sizzling *ghee*, garlic-onions and green
   chillies,
echo nothing but Mogul history.

Remember that night we got caught in the
   monsoon?
You slept motionless
as if you weren't breathing
as if your conscience was clear
like a *moolie*
or the water from the tube-wells in the fields
of rice, pure white,
in the village of Adampur.

Your touch stretched high into the ceiling
and your breath, the spirit of an ancient princess,
was warm and historic,
the taste of *kedgeree*.

All night I remember I listened to your silence;
our distant promises.
And the sound of the rain on a hot tin roof.

XXXII

In what language do you think?
Question on a Swiss Census form

Let's just say this
this for the last time
the last time
this word you loved
let's just say this
this again and this
for a thousand wishes
let's just say this
just this
for the very last time
and nothing else
as if there's
nothing else at all
let's just say this
this word
you've taken to bed
that arouses you
aligns you with
citizenship
or nationality
(whichever means most
on a passport)
let's just say
this word *English*
whatever you perceive
it to be
as if it will hand you
a set of values
which you can embrace
or reject
and your conscience

will be clear
as a crystal ball –
lingual sovereignty
and choice
nothing wrong
with choices, my dear,
it's all part of the trick
pick a card
any card …
and here we are
back at this word
which means so much
and so much that means
sod all.

XXXIV

When the war broke out...

The quiet buzz of the radio
woke me last night –
the intermittent sounds of news, words
and music
bombarding my subconscious mind.

It's the underworld neither here nor there,
just being,
trying to make sense
of this surface reality.

Language came flooding from a midnight sky –
'the imminent' had arrived,
'the inevitable' –
sound bites and political gloss
paving the way now
for fictionality.

'Pictures are coming in',
'the offensive has begun',
'Baghdad woke up to air-raid sirens',
'diplomacy had given way to action'.

Indeed.

And this narrative is intercepted
with a climax,
this 'final scene'
juxtaposed with an array of voices,
reminding us of what has been.

Here's our correspondent in Washington/Kuwait',
'analysis',
'John or Sally with our troops'
and 'Finally…'

Images came to my mind of chess pieces and
     cricket,
of time moving on,
and still we're static,
despite the arts, the guiding scholars
and thousands of poets.

In my head, George Bush (addressing his nation)
and Saddam Hussein (addressing his nation)
stood defiantly
like characters in the grand scheme
of a play.

Amidst all this, the notes of *Moonlight Sonata*
filtered through
touching our hope for humanity.

But oh, Time cover me and all mankind
for the faint tolling of the bell reminds me,
it's tolling for me.

XXXV

...art shows us something about where we are, what we share,
what divides us, the cruelties we commit...
Adrian Searle, The Guardian

You can lead a horse to water
but you can't
for the life of the world
understand the strange complexities
that govern the human mind
like how it is
that this or that came into being
or what this means
if it has a meaning at all
('cause everything has a meaning).
So what now,
that we have blown life to smithereens?
Only the buzzing of the news on CNN
portrays our truths;
only the fluttering of folly and remorse
flicker in the midday heat
where the youths stand purposefully
their hearts ticking
like a song or an imminent bomb
which ever comes first (or last?)
to entice their growing conscience
(or conscious*ness*)
in history, life and politics
in spite of, or as a result of,
'the cruelties we commit'
hidden away by politics –
our crimes safe in our beards.

XXXVI

The rattle of your bangles
and your gold jewellery on the windowsill
woke me that night.

I looked out.
The window ajar in the breeze.

In the darkness the rain fell
drumming incessantly
like the faint calling of a god.

Such was the night.

I could have heard a million voices
clashing with a million gods
defining *clarity* and all that we call *is*.

But I didn't.
I only felt your breathing.

You lay fast asleep like a child
oblivious to the beckoning
of that dying world
crumbling down with the rain.

And I huddled up beside you
as if your touch,
or the contours of your hips,
could cleanse humanity of its sins.

XXXVII

I've decided that I'm going to exchange
my identity for the one defined

by my credit card company –
financial institutions

always know better than us
as to who we are, what we'll earn

and what we can afford.
But keeping up with my new adopted role

is a bit of a strain.
Even my signature is becoming lopsided

falling down from the line
and difficult to keep upright

as if my hands
have become independent of my will.

My choice is not *my* choice.
It's my fate designed by the omnipotent gods

with slick-coloured ties, seated in plush carpeted
    rooms
behind windows with blinds

where money falls from the sky
like confetti on an Indian wedding night.

XXXIX

We were on a late night train
from Calais to Paris.

You were finishing the half-eaten
ham sandwich

we had bought from Waterloo
when out of the blue,

in mid-joke, you paused
as if someone had stepped

over your grave, and your bones
were grinding to dust.

They say that sometimes
we sense a future we didn't plan

arbitrary to all that we call
reason and logic

lying strategically
between life and half-light

like a full moon when
clarity and magic are all,

a sight you can sense,
a brightness,

even in that lull
that cold solitude of the night.

You never did finish that joke
or the ham sandwich

and I remember your eyes
had dropped as if something

deep, whole and abstract
had died inside you.

And amidst the drone
of the engine

and the sadness of your eyes,
we stared out of the window

at the lonely darkness –
reaching to hope

or a promise
in the unmentionable stars –

and a benign universe,
forever changing.

XLIV

No, I read no Poetry now; it might soften me.
Field Marshal Paul von Hindenberg

If I believe that you're real,
all this, that this is love,
if I believe that you're mine
and life is a gentle dove...

The house was silent for quite sometime as we
watched those feats of engineering crumbling
down. The shock and horror of the sight froze us
like icicles on a washing line in January. We
looked on, numb with disbelief, not knowing the
causes of how and why, what philosophy was,
where it had been and how we all fitted in.

And still there was no sound.

Images came and went, searing the retina deep in
the confines of our world as pictures played and
replayed, sometimes in silence, sometimes with
commentary and occasionally in slow motion as if
a frame of the reel might reveal something about
the workings of that illusion, an exploration
underneath our surface reality, the dissecting of a
metrical rhythm, the central point of a heartbeat.

My mother went into the *puja-room* filled with
joss-stick smoke to do the evening *arti* and spent a
lot longer than before, as if the quality of a prayer
is dependent on its length and can flutter itself into
the hands of a god. She placed a sunflower and a
rose I had given her for her birthday – her wish –
next to Hanuman and Krishna, a gift from this

186

world, placing all that she knew, all that she was (and we were), into the wings of fate. She continued for days after that, an earnest ritual she exercised like second nature, all mechanised and perfected, assisted by a range of flowers and sweets. But I knew it wasn't for us, her family, but for humanity this time, the world and all its sins.

Slowly we felt a movement, a tremor, a kind of awakening from sobriety, as if we'd been comatosed for centuries. Daylight came through. Outside the autumnal sun fell and rose as it had for countless years. Nothing changed. And then, within a week, something spoke, nudging us into action, to alertness. Our education and logic subsiding from view. And cold anger emerged.

– Wanted dead or alive, let's smoke them out...

Fictionality interjected with reality both in words and in deeds. It was a sense of calling that's both urgent and dramatic. And an animal instinct getting the better of us, the sound and fury. On our screens we saw leaders standing tall, side by side, united against some common enemies, death and vanity. And the workings of an ego. We looked on, instinctively but clearly mute, listening to speech after speech, defending a call to arms – a bugle call, clashing against the faint tolling of the bell.

– To do nothing is the irresponsible thing.

To do something, anything was paramount. Let words speak, and all our thoughts mould into a ball of fire, for *Readiness was all.*

And we were, all ready. For now it was all revenge, conscience and action colliding like real entities. Ancient gods came out and battled on sovereign ground and celestial bodies moved, rose and died simultaneously, some wide, some narrow, and others not quite forming. And all our crimes in our beards stood like a full moon, all clear, all clarity. And I imagined that they were somewhere in that outer space, just being, as if their presence was all, and all was everything.

– *Action, Hamlet, Action!*

And I remember one night when my mother sat in the *puja-room*, slumped like a sack. She was meditating or had fallen asleep. In the dark she stood out, like a vessel, a body without a spirit or a soul, a keel yearning to find its way back to the universe, the cycle of life and our beginning. And the tear on her cheek, static and motionless, was the size of the world. Next to her the sunflower and the sickly rose lay – wilting in a hope-filled room, all promises, all wishes – as if they too had failed like us and my mother's tear that had died in mid-stream.

– *Hari Rama, hari Krishna, hari Krishna, hari, hari...*

On the screen voices converged as if our life and history depended on it, as if we'd gone back in time and the past, that abstract thought from school, was a physical entity, all relevant. From an aerial view, the end was nigh, a mere moment away, and death was a flicker of reality.

Only your words echoed through, my comfort, like a distant call, a desolate song:

> *...If I believe in your words*
> *and Time crossing the sea,*
> *why is it that I also believe*
> *that Hope will never find me?*

Index

INDEX

195